GOD's GUARANTEES

Promises of God

A Survival Guide for

Walking-the-Walk.

ISBN: 9798842300914

Visit the author at → www.walkingthewalk.us *(.us not .com)*

Message the author at → gkwalkingthewalk@gmail.com

DEDICATED TO

Deborah

Jordan, Elise,

Kyla, Nicole,

Lottie, Banks,

Grady, and Amity

You are loved.

Table of Contents

Author's Suggestion:

This book is topical. You don't have to start at the beginning. Just pick a topic that you think will help you and start there.

<u>PREFACE</u>

Through the years of being a follower of Christ, I've had the peculiar habit of looking up verses that were important to me in various translations, starting with the NASB and moving through others like AMP, ESB, ESV, ERV, LB, NLT, NSB and more.

However, I had a problem. I liked bits of one translation and bits of others. Not being sure what to do with that, I proceeded to piece them together and finish by checking them against the King James Version and Strong's Hebrew and Greek Lexicons, then stored them on my phone and laptop.

Why did I do it? I personally wanted a better understanding of the verses I was studying. The way I saw it, if the verses didn't make sense to me, then I probably wasn't going to apply them to my life.

When I would share these verses with others, forgetting that I was sharing my personal paraphrased versions, I would often get positive feedback, asking what translation I was using.

I think I know why. With nine years of university education and a fairly good command of the English language, I still found it challenging to understand various translations of the Bible. I can guess with confidence that it's the same for other people as well.

All of us have a desire to grasp what God is saying in His Word, but how often do we pass over a phrase or a verse without gaining value from it because its meaning doesn't resonate with our understanding.

With that being said, I in no way want to promote the adherence of any of the paraphrased verses in this book. They are simply presented to help the reader get a better understanding of the verse's meaning.

I would highly recommend comparing the verses presented in this book with your own favourite translation. Or, better yet, there are many Bible apps and Lexicons that are available in phone or computer apps that make it easy (through the touch of the finger) to do your own comparison.

Either way, the goal is for all of us to get the best understanding we can of God's Word into our minds and hearts without deviating from the truth God meant to convey.

I thought it would be good to mention this early in the book because I want you to have <u>my gift</u> that goes hand in hand with this book.

If you would like to receive it then go to my landing page and <u>copy and paste</u> *www.walkingthewalk.us* (*.us* not *.com*) into the <u>URL</u> section at the top of your computer screen.

Then click on <u>Gift To My Readers</u>

It will also put you on <u>my update list</u> to update you on other writing projects I'm working on. You can opt-out anytime.

<u>INTRODUCTION</u>

When I first became a follower of Christ a little over twenty years ago, I brought with me all the thinking and behaviour of the culture around me that I had accumulated through life. I'm sure God was sighing with all he had to deal with when I became his child.

It was a struggle to understand what God was trying to change in me. I didn't grasp how to trust him. I didn't comprehend what loving others meant. After all, it was much easier to find fault in others rather than the good. I didn't understand how to deal with worry, or how to find joy. I wondered why God wasn't answering my prayers. And, when trouble and trials came my way, I just resorted to old habits of dealing with the stresses of life. I didn't know any better.

As I cooperated with God in his attempts to change me, I grew up and matured in my faith, but not without a great deal of struggle.

As I met other believers, whether new or well-seasoned, I found that they too were struggling with much of the same things. As I grew in my faith, I came to realize that what helped my faith grow the most were the promises of God. Those promises excited me and gave me the hope I needed to keep climbing that mountain and not give up.

This book has been written to help you in <u>walking the walk of God</u>. In essence, I consider it an elementary survival guide, nothing fancy in language or substance, but necessary if we want to avoid the cuts, and bruises, and frustrations that accompany our journey of faith. So, may you find it useful in your own journey. If so, then I have succeeded beyond all my expectations.

Before We Dive In

I want you to know something; We have as much of God's blessings or as little of them as we want in our lives. That might seem like a brash thing to say, but it's true – we get to choose.

The world we live in offers us lots of good things. But it's nothing like the amazing things God offers. Plus, what God offers is **absolutely guaranteed** through the promises he made.

> *"God never made a promise that was too good to be true."*
> Dwight L Moody

All through his Word, God gives us promises that seem almost too amazing to be real. But he insists he wouldn't have given them to us if he didn't intend to carry them out.

✢ **Numbers 23:19** → *"Has God ever spoken and failed to carry through? Has he ever promised something and not fulfilled it?"*

I want you to understand something that's foundational to this book and it all centers around his promises.

✢ **2 Peter 1:4** → *God has given us everything we need for living a godly life. He has done this by giving us **incredibly valuable promises**, and by these promises we're able to escape the sin-bent corruptness of this world. In fact, through his promises we're able to participate in God's holy nature and goodness.*

Here's what I want you to see in that verse: All we need for living an abundant and godly life has *already* been given to us through the power of God's Word. And just to make sure we get it; God gives us promises that will help us live it out.

But you know what I see? → Believers asking God for things they've *already* been given...through his promises. I imagine it must frustrate God when he hears us ask, *"Lord, lead me.",* especially when he's *already* said he would. We just need to make a choice to believe what he says and follow him. Or, when we ask – *"Lord, give me the victory."*, especially when God's *already* done it. We just need to apply our will to live in it. Or, how about *"God, give me your peace."* God *already* has. Remember Jesus telling us he's given us his peace?

This book is devoted to looking at some of the promises God has made so we can see what God has *already* guaranteed us to enable us to walk-the-walk of God.

The beautiful thing is → God can carry us through any hurts...habits...or hang-ups we may have, and he uses his promises to help us through them all.

In fact, before we go further, I want to share with you what God promises...*about*...his promises:
Look at these 3 verses:

Psalm 12:6 → *The Lord's promises are <u>absolutely pure</u>, like silver that has been refined in a furnace and purified seven times over.*

This verse is making the point that if you refined silver seven times, you could pretty much be certain that you had the purest silver money could buy. God's promises are just like that – perfect, pure, dependable, the very best you could hope for.

Psalm 138:2 → *God's promises are <u>backed</u> by all of the honor of his name.*

Is there any other name that's higher or more honourable than God's name that could be used as a guarantee that he'll make good on his promises?

1 Kings 8:56 → *<u>Not one word</u> has ever failed in all the wonderful promises he has given.*

That's an amazing promise. Think about it -- *"Not one word!"* That basically leaves no room for doubt. *'Not one word'* means...not one single, solitary word of God's promises has ever failed to come true.

People often casually speak empty and idle words. But God doesn't. Each and every word he has ever spoken is full of life and power. In fact, his Word contains within itself the power to bring itself to pass. Read this guarantee:

✦ Isaiah 55:11 → *My word will not return empty, without results. It always accomplishes the purposes for which I sent it.*

If we can't hang our hat on these verses, then we might as well stop here.....No, don't stop here. That was just a figure of speech. There are wonderful promises still to come.☺

Let me say one more thing before we move on. → If we want God's promises to yield powerful results in our lives, then we can't just be satisfied with *knowing* what they say. We have to chew on those promises, believe them with our whole heart, and then live them out in our lives. Just reading God's promises in this book won't change your life, but putting them to use and living them out will. That's called *abiding in the Word.*

So, let's do some digging and stake our claim on some gold nuggets of God's promises. (Ok...I agree...that's cheesy)

Note:

Just so you don't miss it.

This book was not necessarily intended to be read from front to back.

Instead, it is laid out in topics. So, you don't have to start at the beginning.

Just pick a topic that you think may help you and start there.

BLESSINGS
What God Guarantees about Blessings

We are too prone to engrave our trials in marble and write our blessings in sand. — Charles Spurgeon

Do you know what God's favorite pastime is? Doing good things for us. God is always in a favorable mood. He wants to bless his people he loves with good things. As far as God's concerned, he wants us to experience his goodness every day, everywhere we turn.

Here's the thing though: There are a few contingencies that God mentions that we need to apply in our lives in order to experience his blessings. He seems to be pretty specific about them, too. And, if we don't know these keys that unlock the doors to his blessings....well, we just might miss out on some of them.

Let me mention a few of these keys, because if you know them and practice them until they become a regular part of your life, then a ton of blessings will be unlocked for you. Just read on and you'll see for yourself.

Ok, I know I'll get some flak for it if I don't say this first.
I'm not necessarily a *"name it and claim it"* kind of person, but when it comes to God's promises, if God offers us a guarantee, then I'll take it. So, should you. Because any promise God gives is bound to be good for us.

I think we would do well to remember something, however. →
God is God, and we're not. So, if he, as our heavenly father and caretaker, chooses to *allow* hardship, or difficulties, or sickness

from the enemy to invade our lives, then we need to understand that they too can *become* blessings. We just need to see them the way God sees them...through his lens. He can turn what seems like lemons, into lemonade. If we can accept that simple idea, then we're well on our way to blessings flowing into our lives.

There's an old saying among the cowboys of the Old West:
Glass half empty or glass half full. Either way you look at it, you won't be going thirsty.

That's a great way to see the situations in our lives, isn't it? Whether our life is half empty or half full, either way, we won't be losing out on God's blessings.

You might be thinking → *"How can hardships be blessings?"*

Well, maybe you'd agree that many of us fail to see our lives as God sees them. We fail to look at our circumstances through the same lens that God does. We usually see life from our own perspective, and so when bad stuff happens to us, or we don't get what we were hoping for from God....well, we kind of sulk or throw a hissy fit. Come on, don't tell me you don't. We all do it. We just do it in different ways, and I bet God smiles when he sees it.

Look at how God describes his way of thinking and doing things:

Isaiah 55:8 → *My thoughts (the way I see things) are nothing like your own thoughts (how you see things), and my way of doing things is not like your way of doing things.*

If we can start to see our circumstances (whether good or bad) the way God sees them, we'll handle life a whole lot better...pardon my grammar☺. The point I'm making is that blessings may not always be all the good stuff we want in our lives.

The secret to happiness is to count your blessings while others are adding up their troubles. William Penn

Everyone wants blessings from God, right? However, before we go any further, we really need to get a handle on something:

What exactly is a *blessing*?

I find a lot of people use the words *'blessed'* or *'blessing'* in their conversations, but when I ask them what the word means, they often struggle to define it.

So, here's a description of what blessings from God are:

1.) Blessings, according to the Bible, is God's supernatural favor poured out into our lives. But they are more than just good things that befall us, they can also be adversity and hardships.

2.) Blessings can be material in substance or spiritual.

3.) Blessings are also given to us so we can share them with others in return.

4.) Blessings can be in the present, here on earth, or in the future, in God's heaven.

Let's look at some blessings God guarantees us:

Now listen, this may not be the best passage to start off with because it's kinda' long, but **don't pass it by. It's important.** There are a bunch of truly astounding blessings that will fill your life with amazing things if you pay attention and do what's mentioned in these verses. In fact, God *guarantees* they will not only be in your life, they will chase you down until they find you. In other words, you can't escape them. Check it out:

Deuteronomy 28:1-3 (Moses, the mouthpiece of God, speaking to God's people) → *If you fully do what God tells you to do* (meaning - completely obey him) *and you're careful to keep his instructions...you will experience all of these blessings. They will chase you down and grab onto your life, and they will be yours if you listen to God and do what he tells you to do.*

- *You will be blessed in the city, and you will be blessed in the field.* (meaning→ whether you live in a city or in a rural setting, it doesn't matter to God, he'll chase you down to bless you.)

- *Your families will be blessed, as well as your crops and your herds. They will be blessed as well.*

Note: (If you're a farmer then this promise would apply, and if you're not a farmer, it still applies. Why? Because at the time this passage was written, the main form of business and wealth was their crops and herds. Today, it's our work, our businesses, and our financial holdings. These are the things that God will bless in our lives.)

- *Your baskets of food and your breadboards will be blessed.* (meaning→ you'll have no lack of food and plenty to eat. You won't go hungry.)

- *Whatever you do and wherever you go, you will receive blessings.*

- *When your enemies attack you, they will attack you from one direction, but they will run and flee from you in seven different directions.* (meaning → Your enemies, if you have any, will intend to hurt you, but God will scatter them, and you'll remain unharmed.)

- *In everything you undertake, God will guarantee blessings on it.*

- *He will fill your storehouse with grain.*
  Note: (We may not have a barn or a storehouse for grain, which in those days was like a bank, and the grain was like their money. What God is saying here is that your savings and investments will be blessed.)

- *He will bless you wherever you live.*

- *God will make you his own special people, if you hold onto (keep) his instructions in your heart and are careful to obey everything he tells you to do. Then everyone around you will see that you are blessed as God's special people, and they will be amazed.*
  Note: (Being God's own special people means you're under his special protection and blessing. You're his children and he will personally go out of his way to take good care of you and to give you good things.)

- *Do these things and the Lord God will give you great prosperity through your family, your livestock, and your land.*
  Note: (Again, we may not have livestock or crops, but the meaning for us today is that God will bless us with abundance in our work, our family-life, and our holdings.)

- *He will open his treasure house where he keeps his blessings and send <u>rain</u> when your land needs it.*

    Note: (For most of us today, because we don't have farms, God is saying he will bless your way of making a living, especially when you have needs.)

- *He will bless everything you do. E<u>verything</u>!*

- *You will lend money to others, but you'll <u>never have to borrow</u> from them.*

- *He will make you the head and not the tail and you will <u>be on the top, not the bottom</u> <u>if</u> you truly listen to God's instructions and carefully do them.*

    Note: (What it's saying about being the head and not the tail, or being on top, not the bottom, is that you'll do well and never fail at your endeavors. You'll always be on top.)

- ***But*** *<u>you must make sure</u> you don't turn aside or turn away from any of the instructions God gives....*

Whew...that was long, wasn't it? Don't worry, it's the only long one in this book...but it's amazing. If you had one passage to hang your blessings on, this is it.

Think about it. If we just relied on these promises alone, we would have an incredible life. I mean, God went out of his way to spell out for us all the amazing things he was looking forward to doing for his people back then and for us today. God never changes, so we can receive these guarantees today as well.

By the way, God doesn't have to do any of those things for us. He could have just said, *"Do what I tell you to do. It's for your own good."* But instead, he added all these fantastic blessings...just because he wanted to. And then he said that you won't be able to escape them. They'll chase you down and fill your life. You know why? Because God's <u>always</u> good to us <u>all</u> of the time.

<u>**You may be thinking**</u> → *"Well I don't think what's in those verses is going to happen to me. I follow God and I never see that stuff happening in my life."*

I get it, but it's God who's making these guarantees. So, who are we to argue with God? If he wants to do those amazing things for us, what right do we have to doubt it? But maybe that's really the problem...we *doubt* it...hmmm.☺ Listen, all we have to do is make sure we listen and consistently obey...carefully. Then receive what God wants to give us. It may take faith on your part, but that's what we're supposed to be living by anyway – faith.

Here's a question for you: If we're *not* seeing those blessings happening in our lives, then what is it we might be missing? My answer is pretty basic.→ Look at the beginning, middle and end of that passage. If we're doing those things mentioned, then we're <u>guaranteed</u> all those wonderful blessings. God promises it, plain and simple. **So, check yourself.** Are there any *'blessing-blockers'* in your life? If you're not sure, ask God. He'll show you. Are you doing what he tells you to do? If not, then start. Then, wait for all those amazing blessings he said he would give us. He won't let you down. He lives up to his Word.

People say: *"Well, those blessings were meant for people in the Old Testament. It was based on obeying the Law. We live in the New Testament era of Grace.* That's all true. Yes, they were given to God's people in the Old Testament, but God never changes and neither does his Word. It's the same for us in the New Testament era. So, do what that passage says and let those blessings chase you down and fulfil themselves in your life.

You wanna know something that's strange?
Many people think God doesn't want them to have good things in their lives and that if he even blesses them at all, then he'll be stingy about it. They think that he'll be annoyed with them if they ask him for stuff. They think God's only pleased when they only have just enough, barely enough to get by. *"After all"*, they say, *"that's not what life's about."*

But that's not what God's about! All through the Bible, we find God expressing his desire to lavish upon his *obedient* children more and more blessings to make life good for them...more than they could possibly imagine.

You know what? God wants us to enjoy life, enjoy each other, enjoy his creation, and enjoy him. That was his original plan for us way back in the garden...until it all went kaput.

But some might say → *"Look at Jesus. He didn't have his own home, or money, or even a bed to call his own. He had virtually nothing. Shouldn't we live like him?"*

Well, Jesus is God's *'selfie'*. Right? I mean, Colossians 1:15 says that Jesus is the visible image of our invisible God, and that God was pleased to live fully in Jesus. So, if you think about it, it's God and Jesus who want you to have all those blessings in the passage we just read. It's his kingdom and he wants to share all the good things in his kingdom with us. He even goes to the trouble of *describing in detail* the things he wants to give us and do for us. Just review the passage we just covered.

If **you're struggling and feeling like you're not worthy** to receive all the great things mentioned in that passage, then understand this. → You are God's child *if* you've been adopted into his family. And get this...you've been adopted by a King, the King of the Universe, who has a lot of good stuff in his kingdom that he wants to share with us to enjoy.

And not only that, but our king is very wealthy with all kinds of possessions, and he's *always* in a favorable, generous mood. You'll never catch him having a bad day. He just loves to give good things to his kids – that's us. It's one of his favorite things to do. The Bible says that all good gifts come down to us from our Father in Heaven (See James 1:17) He makes that plain all through the Bible. So, believe it.

If you're struggling with obedience to God, then stop messing with his blessing. → Do what he tells you to do at the beginning, middle, and end of that passage we just covered, and open up your hands to receive. *If* we do our part, God will do his. He guarantees it.

🌲 **Did you know that God's desire to bless us with very good things is even greater than a parent's desire to bless his or her own children?**

✦ **Matt 7:11** Jesus speaking → *If you, as messed up, flawed human beings know how to give good things to your children, then how much more will your perfect Father in heaven give good things to those who ask him for them?*

Two things worth mentioning here.

1.) Notice the word "more". In Greek, it's a quantitative word with the implication of, *'How much more in quantity and good intention will God give good things to his children than even you as parents give to your own kids?'* I would suggest you claim that guarantee. It's yours.

2.) Notice the word "ask". Even Jesus here is suggesting that we ask for good things. You might think that it's selfish to do so, but he doesn't. So, ask, because the reality is that if you don't ask, like he tells you to, then you won't receive. Plus, it robs God of the joy to make his children happy, just like any parent wants. Are you going to rob God of that joy? Just say "*No.*" ☺

Has your child (if you have one) ever asked you for good things? Doesn't it feel right, and doesn't it make you happy to give it to them? Well, you're now a child of royalty, and the king is your heavenly Father...so start asking. He's waiting.

I think many of God's children have a hard time accepting their new ancestry. They don't think of themselves as part of a royal family. But the thing is, Jesus knows he's a king, and he expects us to know that we're heirs along with him. He made us co-heirs to his kingdom, at least that's what God says in his Word. **So, if God believes we're royalty**, then we should believe it too.

🌲 If you doubt whether God is serious about you asking him for stuff, then read this next promise:

✦ **John 16:24** Jesus speaking→ *Ask me for things* (with faith backing it up) *and you will receive it, so that **your joy** may be full.*

What's the point of us 'asking' in this promise? So that it will give *us* a bunch of joy. I know, it could sound selfish if we don't look at it the way God sees it...but, hey, I didn't say it. The King of Heaven did. So, start asking him for stuff.

But here's the catch: Read this next verse.

✦ **James 4:3** → *When you ask for things from God, you end up <u>not</u> receiving them, because your <u>motives</u> are wrong. You ask for things only to fulfill your own wants and desires, to gratify your own pleasure.*

You might be thinking → *"Wait a second, don't those two verses contradict each other? I mean, first Jesus tells us to ask for things to make us happy. And now the apostle James is telling us not to do that because we're being selfish. What's the deal?"* (Maybe you don't talk that way, but that's how I'm writing it.)☺

It all comes down to the <u>motives</u> behind the asking. There's nothing wrong with asking for stuff that will make us happy, but **if** it's just a spiritual wishbone to fulfil our own self-centered pleasure rather than fulfil the overall will and pleasure of God in giving it to us, then we may not receive an answer.
<u>Example</u>: If we ask for a Mercedes convertible, rather than a car to get us to work, then we may not get what we want, right?

Do you know what God's original intent for humanity was, way back in the Garden of Eden? It was to supply *all* our needs and take really good care of us. But the first two humans on this earth kind of messed that up with wrong desires and motives.

God's original plan when he created mankind was for them to live on this earth as happy, stress-free people, having a beautiful relationship with him, letting him provide for them and protect them. He provided them with trees and plants to feed them. All they had to do was gather and eat. They didn't even have to sow crops or toil to earn a living. God never intended them to struggle just to barely make it. He simply wanted them to enjoy living in his blessings...to let him provide for them in abundance.

But you know what the first two people on earth did? Because God gave them a *free-will*, they chose to throw it all away. They were the first people to not read the Apple terms and conditions. Now we're all paying for it. All they had to do was follow his instructions and receive good things from him. But they chose to turn away from him and go their own way. Still, over and over again, through the centuries, God waited for them to come back to him. Instead, they refused.

God never gave up on his original design, though. He created a new plan to restore mankind to his original blessings once again. It would be at just the right time, when his chosen one, Jesus, the Saviour of humanity, would come into the world, born as a man, to live as a human, and be put to death as a criminal on a Roman cross, all to pay the price for our rebellion.

But God couldn't wait for the Messiah to come so he could once again start blessing his children after they fell. So, in the meantime (two thousand years *before* Christ came), he made an agreement with his people (a covenant). → He said if they would trust him and obey him (for their own good) then he would provide for them and protect them, take good care of them, and bless them with good things, just as he did in the beginning, with his original plan.

Do you know what happened? → Time and time again God provided opportunities for his people to accept this new agreement and just step back into his sphere of blessings. But they repeatedly chose to step out of it.

People blame God for terrible things happening – adversity, tragedies, calamities. *"After all"*, they say, *"if God's in control, then it must be him that caused it."*

The truth is, mankind won't let God control things. They continually get in the way, stepping out of his sphere of blessings. However, God repeatedly tells us the outcome for doing what he tells us to do, and the outcome for *not* doing what he tells us to do. And then, you know what he does? → He lets us *choose* which outcome we want. For example, read the verse below. **It's sort of a promise...or...a curse.**

Deuteronomy 30:19&20 (Moses speaking for God to his people) → *Today I am giving you a choice - between life or death, between blessings or calamity. It is yours to make. If you choose the life God offers, it brings blessings. If you choose the path that leads away from God, the path that leads to spiritual death, it will bring ruin. So, choose life. You can make this choice* _by_ loving God and consistently doing what he tells you to do (for your own good), _and by sticking close to him; for he is your life_ (the abundant life your desire)...

Put this in your backpack as you walk through life:
Wanna know how God works?

* He's God, so he makes the rules...because he knows what's best for us, what will keep us from hurting ourselves.

* He tells us what to do so he can bless us, protect us, and keep us from ruining our lives. Then he lets us _choose_ what we want to do.

* If we choose to live the way he tells us to, then we can bask in the flow of his blessings.

* If we choose _not_ to live his way, then we lose out on those blessings.

But just remember if things don't go well for us...it's not God's fault. Don't think, "_God did this to me!_" That's not the way God works. God doesn't withhold blessings and good things from those who are careful to do what he tells them to do. And, even if we aren't obedient, God is still so kind that he even spares the disobedient for as long as possible, hoping they'll turn back to him.

✥ **Exodus 34:6** God speaking→ _I am God, the one who is full of mercy_ (not giving you what you actually deserve) _and full of compassion, and slow to get angry, who shows great love and faithfulness toward you._

✥ **2 Peter 3:9** → _God is very, very patient toward us when we ignore him and go astray. He does not want any of us to be ruined or destroyed, but rather that we would change our ways._

Lucky for us, God grades on the cross, not the curve. Right?
1 cross + 3 nails = 4-given.

Remember this: God's heart is always for us, not against us. He wants us to do well in life...to live and prosper and enjoy his company. He doesn't want us to lose our way and get off his path. He knows the troubles it brings. That's why he gave us his instructions – to help us *stay* on the right path that leads straight to his blessings.

Bottom-line: If we would just do what he says, then we'd enjoy good days of blessings. And remember, even though it may be hard to understand, good days can still include adversity, hardship, and struggles. Think about it, how many times have we said something like this, *"Man, that was the hardest time in my life, but it was also the best."*

"Yeah, yeah...enough of that obedience stuff. Give me more of the guarantees!"

Fine...I will.

But first, do you remember those "promises *about* his promises" that I mentioned at the beginning of this book? That his promises are *purer than the purest silver* money can buy, and that he backs up his promises with *all of the honor of his name*, and that *not one word* has ever failed in any of the promises he's made?

You know what that tells us? We've got it made, because in that long passage we just covered a few pages back, with all those amazing blessings; if God guarantees them, then he'll do them...plain and simple. There's nothing stopping them from happening except perhaps one thing...*us*. We can mess up God's plans to bless us. So, don't be messin' with his blessin'. Got it?

Try it...You'll Like It

Psalm 34:8 → *Taste* and *see for yourself,* try it and find out that *God wants to give you good things* (Hebrew meaning - to give you good things that are pleasant, that will help you thrive, not just survive, but thrive and prosper and do well in life).

That's what we have to do...we have to taste it and try it out. We need to find out for ourselves just how good God's promises are. What will it require from us? → Believing in what God says. Simply believe. Stop doubting. I mean, think about it, believing is no harder than doubting anyway...so why not believe.

Here's one way to do it → **ABC** his guarantees:

<u>Agree</u> with what God says – that he wants to give you good things to help you do well in life, that he wants you to taste it and find out for yourself.

<u>Believe</u> in your heart that God never lies. If he says he intends to bless you with good things, then he'll do it.

<u>Confess</u> it over again, to feed your faith and starve your doubts.

Here's one more letter, and it's pretty important, I mean really important!→ "**D**" stands for *Do* what he tells us to do, being careful to follow his instructions. And don't be mediocre about it, either. Be diligent. No one likes to hear this truth, but it's the most important key to unlocking the door to God's blessings.

What's the big deal about the "D"?

Well, let me point out <u>3 things</u> that are crucial in order for God's guarantees to come true in our lives:

1.) <u>God makes it clear what he expects from us in doing the 'D'.</u>→ To pay attention to his voice, to listen to his instructions, and then continually <u>*do*</u> them. That's what opens the door for him to bless us. They're for our well-being anyway. So, guess what? That's what we need to do *if* we want God's blessings to flow into our lives – Do the "**D**".

And always remember this → His instructions aren't there to stifle us, deprive us, or to keep us under his thumb. They are there to help us avoid ruining our lives, to help us *stay* in the sphere of his blessings.

<u>You might be thinking</u> → *"But, it's just too hard to do what God tells me to do!"*

You know what I want you to do? Read these three promises:

✧ **<u>1 John 5:3</u>** → *Loving God means doing what he tells us to do, and really, his instructions are <u>not burdensome or hard for us at all</u>.*

✧ **<u>Mathew 11:30</u>** Jesus speaking→ *The burden that I ask you to bear is <u>easy to carry</u>, and the instructions I yoke you to are <u>easy to do</u>.*

✦ **Proverbs 10:22** → *God's blessings will make you happy and help you to prosper in life, <u>without painful toil for it</u>.*

What are those verses telling us? That doing what he tells us to do is not hard...at all. So, no whining...do the **"D"**.

But watch out! Don't slip on this one thing:
You know what I've noticed? Many people don't know God's instructions very well, and that just might be a *'blessing-blocker'* for them. I mean, just think about it, if we don't really know the instructions given to us by God...how are we going to be careful to follow them?

✦ **Hosea 4:6** → *My people are being ruined, pummelled, and destroyed because they don't know, or understand, or follow my instructions.*

So, here's what I recommend. → Pick a passage in the four gospels or the letters of Paul, John, or Peter and just read one or two verses. Write yourself two or three questions on how you'd apply it to your life...and then write down exactly what you're going to do to make it happen that week. They have to be concrete steps. It might be one or two steps. That's all. Ponder it and think about it periodically throughout the day and evening and then *act* on it. Do this every day...without fail and you'll be amazed at how it helps you remember what God tells you to do.

What I find helpful is to copy and paste the verse(s) into my phone and look at it throughout the day or week, asking myself questions, and praying out the verse(s). Usually, I tend to forget them, but because I've stored them on my phone app, I can go back to them any time I want and review them.

By the way, there are lots of phone and computer apps these days that allow us to read God's Word and compare different translations to get a better understanding of what God's saying. And, there are apps that, with one press of the finger, we can look at the Greek or Hebrew meaning of a word. And, there are apps that we can copy and paste verses to, so we can look at them whenever we want to.

Reading and studying God's Word in this day and age has never been easier. We just gotta do it. Right?

2.) The blessings that come from doing the "D" are to be shared with others.

✦ **2 Corinthians 9:8** → *God is always able and <u>more than ready</u> to give you <u>abundant blessings</u>, so that you'll <u>always have</u>, in all circumstances, <u>more than enough of everything</u>, as well as <u>plenty left over to share</u> with others.*

That's amazing! Did you know God's not just ready, but more than ready to give us abundant blessings? We'll have more than enough...not just enough, but <u>more than enough</u>!

But, don't just look at blessings as something just for you. That's the amazing thing about God; he gives us <u>more than enough</u>, so that we can *share* with others. So, remember to do that when God blesses you. Don't just receive the blessing and leave it at that. <u>Look around</u> for someone to share it with.
- If you're financially blessed by God, share some of it.
- If you're blessed with more than enough to buy groceries, think about sharing some of them.
- If you've been blessed with healing, share some comfort, that God showed you, with someone else.

You get the idea, right? If God's been generous with us, then we shouldn't be stingy in any way...<u>give some of it away</u>.

Also, notice that in that verse is the guarantee that God's ready to give you *<u>abundant</u>* blessings. That word *<u>abundant</u>* in the Greek means – to superabound in quantity and quality, to have in excess, to have over-and-above in abundance. Sooooo...what are we waiting for? Ask. He's ready. Just don't forget to share it with others. Then he'll give you more.

🌲 **Here's another guarantee that's really important.**

✦ <u>**Luke 6:38**</u> This is Jesus speaking to us → *If you <u>give to others</u> <u>generously</u>, then <u>generous gifts will be given back</u> to you* (meaning - you will be given <u>much</u> in return). *In fact, you will be given so* *much in return that you won't be able to hold onto it and it will spill over into your lap, so to speak. The way that you give to others is exactly the way God will give to you.*

That is a huge promise! Huge! The question is...what are *you* going to do with it? Are you going to ABC(D) it?
<u>A</u>gree with God that you'll give generously to others,
<u>B</u>elieve it in your heart that he will generously give back to you.
<u>C</u>onfess it with faith, with confidence, that God will do what he says and come through for you?. Feed that faith and starve that doubt!☺
And remember what the "<u>D</u>" is for. → <u>D</u>o what he tells you to do in that verse. Start giving more. Be more generous...not just to get a lot back in return, but out of gratitude for all that God's given you. Then watch what happens. It may be immediate, or it may be a month or a year. Just watch.

Don't forget the very last sentence in that promise→ *'The <u>way</u> that you give to others is <u>exactly</u> the way God will give to you.'*
That can be exciting or it can be unnerving, because if you're *not* giving generously, then you *won't* be getting much from God. But, if you're giving generously to others, God guarantees to give back to you more than enough. It will spill over. Your cup runneth over. That's called *"blessings"*.

This may sound silly, but an easy way to be generous is...to be generous, knowing full well that you won't lose out on anything because God will then give back to you <u>more than enough</u> so you'll be able to give generously again.
In other words, God will supply the stuff for you to become generous with. So, there's nothing to be stingy about. It's a win-win for you...and others.

So, give generously and then <u>watch</u> what God does. I can tell you from my own experience that I often missed what God gave back to me in return. I didn't make the connection because it was a month or a year later when it came. But as I reflected on that particular blessing that I received, I realized it wasn't just happenstance, it was God giving back in return. I just wasn't watching for it. Now I watch. So can you.

3.) <u>Don't treat God like a genie in a bottle</u>. Don't do the "D" just to get something in return.

Yes, God tells us to <u>ask</u> for blessings (*if*) we're being faithful to <u>do</u> what he tells us in his Word. However, if we're *not* being faithful, then we shouldn't expect much from God in return. Just keep in mind he knows our hearts and our thoughts, so we might as well get our <u>motives</u> right from the very beginning.

And by the way, there's nothing wrong with wanting financial, physical, and materialistic blessings. If it were wrong, then God wouldn't have gone out of his way to mention all he wants to do for us in those areas. He'd be disappointed if we didn't get excited and want them in our lives. But let's <u>do a heart check</u>. What's our motive in asking for what we're asking for?

Ok, read this next verse: You could kind of treat it as a warning and you can treat it as a promise too, *if* you do the opposite.

<u>Deuteronomy 5:29</u> God speaking → *Oh, if only they would have <u>a heart like I desire</u>; that they would <u>listen</u> to me and willingly <u>do</u> all that I tell them to do. <u>If</u> they did, they would <u>prosper,</u> and be blessed, and <u>everything would go well for them</u> and their descendants.*

You can see the *warning* in the verse, right? But how would you claim this as a promise of blessing? Something like this → *"God, you say that you yearn to have children that listen to you and obey your instructions. And if they would do this, they would prosper, and all would go well for them. I'm your child, and I'm listening to you, and I have been careful to obey you, knowing it will help me. So, prosper me, God, and make things go well for me. I receive and wait for these things from you..."*

Hold on to this guarantee. It's a good one:

<u>Psalm 84:11</u> (in the last part of the verse) → *God will not hold back or refuse to give <u>any</u> good thing to those <u>who continually do what is right before him</u>.*

This is so important. We can't miss this point _if_ we want God's blessings to be poured out on our lives. What would hold back good things from flowing into our lives? I think you've got the answer already. → <u>Not</u> doing what he tells us to do.

Always keep in mind that doing what God tells us to do is peppered all through the Bible and is deeply entwined with him blessing us. God knows what will help us and what will hurt us. So, the instructions in his Word are only for our good. If you're struggling with this issue, take care of it asap so it doesn't become a _'roadblock'_ to blessings in your life. In other words, _**Stop messing with the blessing.**_ → Do what he tells you to do.

You know what? The enemy isn't afraid of people who go to church, or who read the Bible, or attend Bible studies. What he's afraid of is people starting to look like Jesus and that will only happen when they <u>consistently</u> do what God tells them to do. That's what Jesus did, and that's what God expects us to do.

<u>Put this in your backpack as you're walking through life</u>:
When God tells us to do stuff in his Word, he's giving us boundaries and protection to keep us safe. Protection? From what? From ourselves...and from the enemy of our souls. So, when you read his instructions in his Word...just do it. **It's the safest way to live on this crazy messed-up planet**.

And here's another point as well: God blesses us because of _his_ faithfulness, not just ours. But if we act unfaithfully, like disobedient children, then, even though God is faithful and wants to bless us, he just might put us in the corner...a time-out, so to speak, along with no dessert. In other words – no blessings. But, as soon as we turn back to him, and get back on his path, we find him waiting to give us good things again.

Would you agree that God's not vindictive...that he doesn't want to punish us or make us pay when we do wrong? That's just not the heart of God. But, like a good father, he'll use discipline to teach us how to live so we can remain in his sphere of protection and blessings. And sometimes his discipline hurts.

<u>So, here's the bottom-line on all of this</u>:

Everything that God tells us to do is for our good. He's not trying to keep us under his thumb or squeeze the joy of living out of us, nor make life hard for us. He wants us to do what he says because he truly wants us to have an *abundant* life, to bless us with good things. He doesn't want the '*roadblocks*' to get in the way. He wants his children to do really well. I'll say it again and again: God is always good to us...*all* of the time.

And keep in mind that when we ignore God and just do what we want, without regard to what he wants for us, then we've just put a '*roadblock*' in the path of his blessings? In fact, if we're not paying attention, those roadblocks may seem to us like God's just making life hard for us. But it's usually not his fault...it's usually ours. He didn't leave our side...we just got side-tracked and left his side. We create the *blessing-blockers*, not God. We weren't paying attention to follow his instructions.

You might be thinking → *"It's just too hard to live the way God wants us to."*

I get it...sometimes the paths to his blessings aren't easy. But I want you to know it will <u>always</u> take you to good places. That's God's heart.

I've always liked this phrase→ *"May you live all the days of your life." (Jonathan Swift)*
You know what I find sad about that statement? Many of us don't do it. We limit our lives by not believing in God's promises. We limit ourselves by not doing what he tells us to do. We lose out on his amazing blessings that make life so much better. So, you know what I suggest we do? Let's really live life...<u>God's way</u> and enjoy the abundant guarantees that come with it.

Here's an amazing guarantee for us to receive...*but* it has two contingencies:

Psalm 31: 19 → *How <u>huge</u> is your goodness toward us, God, and how <u>huge</u> is the abundance of good things you've stored up for those who live with deep reverence and respect for you. You pour out those blessings on those who trust you for* *help, and guidance, blessings, and protection. And you bless them with these good things before a watching world.*

Did you catch it? God just doesn't want to give us a *few* good things to make our lives better, he wants to give us a _huge_ number of good things. The Hebrew meaning for that word _huge_ is *'exceedingly abundant, plenteous, a great amount in quantity and quality'*. It's not only the amount, but it's also the quality of the blessings that God intends to pour out on our lives. Nothing but the best for his kids.

Not only that, but the Hebrew word for _God's goodness_ in that promise is *'chesed' which* means he wants to give us things that are pleasant, things that will help us thrive, not just survive, but thrive, and prosper, and do well in life. Man, that sounds good. Who doesn't want that, right?

But there are two contingencies involved. Don't worry, they're simple.
1) The first contingency is living our lives with *deep reverence* and *respect* toward God. Some Bible translations call it *'the fear of the Lord'*. You don't hear that being preached by many churches these days, and I can understand why. Having a fear of God doesn't sound very good to most people, but that's what that verse says God wants from us.

Lucky for us though, *fearing God* is less fearsome than it sounds. It literally means to live with a deep reverence and respect for God. And you know what that will produce in our lives? → obedience to his instructions and godly living. Why is that? Because the meaning of the Hebrew phrase *'fearing God'* includes using serious caution and self-evaluation to avoid anything that would offend God or defame his name. Doing that leads to obedience and godly living.
And here's what God guarantees us → If we live with a deep respect and reverence toward him**,** he'll bless us with a *huge* amount of good things that will help us do well in life.

2) The second contingency is to really, truly *trust God* for his help, and guidance, blessings, and protection. When we do that and not seek them from other sources, God promises to honor us by 'pouring out' wonderful blessings into our daily living.

Plus, those blessings will be so huge and so amazing that people around us will notice. That's what that promise says. They won't be able to miss it. That's how great his blessings will be.

Why does God want people out there in the world to see the huge blessings of his goodness in our lives? Because he wants them to see how good he is so that perhaps they will turn to him. So, if you think about it, one reason we should want to prosper and be blessed is to show the world around us that there is a God in heaven who is good to his kids. Then maybe they'll want what we have. Right?

Sadly, that often isn't the case. Instead of seeing God's kids fully blessed and living obedient, godly lives, as a result of having a deep respect for God, the world out there sees too many ill-disciplined believers, who lack understanding, living lives of despondency, deficiency, and disappointment. You know what that does to God's reputation? Yikes!!! That's not what God intended for us. Romans 2:24 talks about God's kids conducting their lives with such disregard toward him, that the name of God is <u>blasphemed</u> (spoken ill of, with disdain and reproach) by <u>un</u>believers.

Let's not be one of them. Let's receive a huge amount of amazing blessings from God because of how we live...so the whole world can see how good God is.

Keep this in mind → There are limits on the goodness of God. But the limits aren't on God's side...they're on our side. We can limit how much of God's goodness will be poured out into our lives when we disregard his voice, when we lack understanding of his Word, when we choose not to do what he instructs, or when we doubt God and lack the faith to receive his promises. <u>It's an easy fix though</u>. We can pull the *limits* off of God's blessings. How? Just do the opposite of those things. God's waiting to pour out those blessings in front of a watching world. All we have to do is cooperate.

 And one more thing:

We need to remember to be <u>thankful</u> and express our thanks to God when he pours out those blessings on us.

⬥ **Psalm 50:23** God speaking → *The person who offers up the sacrifice of thanksgiving to me, that person glorifies me.*

Notice the word '_sacrifice_' in that verse. It means to give up something for the sake of another. Does God need our thanks or the glory? Nope. He knows that it's more beneficial to us than to him if we do it. Why is that? Well, what are we sacrificing when we offer up our thanks? We're giving up a little bit of our time, a little bit of our 'self-centeredness' (because we're giving God the credit, not us), and a little bit of our comfort zone. So, I guess it's true: *"Gratitude is the best attitude"* to have.

And notice this next verse. It ties in with all the blessings we receive from God:

⬥ **1Thessalonians 5:16 says to** → *Be thankful in all of the circumstances in your life, no matter what the situation may be, because this is what God wants. It's his will for you.*

I think that's pretty clear, don't you? No confusion in that verse. When it says it's God's *will* for us, that means we should do it. No complaining or wallowing with indifference. And if the going gets rough for us in life...what should we do? Yup. – Be thankful.

An old country proverb says:
"Happy are those who see beautiful things where other people see nothing."
A thankful heart does that.

PEACE
What God Promises You

"Peace doesn't come from finding a lake with no storms. It comes from having Jesus in the boat." John Ortberg

For he himself is our peace. (Ephesians 2:4)

We all want to live in peace, don't we? No one wants strife, or worry, or anxiety, or fear to cloud their life. So, what exactly does God guarantee us about peace?

A good place to start are some *Let/Don't Let* promises.

John 14:27 Jesus speaking → *"I am leaving you with this gift – peace of mind* (your thoughts) *and peace of heart* (your emotions). *And my peace that I give you* (the peace that comes from me) *is not the same as the peace the world offers. So, receive it, and **don't let** your hearts be troubled or afraid.*

Did you notice that we don't have to work at getting the peace that Jesus is offering? It's a gift. There's no effort involved. We just simply receive it...by believing. It's a choice we need to make though, to receive the gift...receive his peace. If we don't make that choice, then we may be walking around without it.

How do you know if you've received it? You'll know because you'll have his peace inside you. It will be different than the usual peace living in this world brings. That's what Jesus said. Deep down, you'll know that it's supernatural.

Something we _do_ have to work at, however, is not letting our hearts return to mulling over what's troubling us. That's the hard part, isn't it? So, how do we do that? → It's done by making a choice – a choice to _not let_ our hearts be troubled, and instead, capture those troubling thoughts and emotions every time they appear. Then, what do we do? We give them back to God, releasing them into his hands, letting go once again. It's an ongoing process, over and over again. The more we do it, the easier it becomes.

You probably already knew that, but it's good to hear it again...and again...and again. Why? Because it's hard to do. We often give our worries and fears to God, then we take them back again - out of God's hands and back into our own. We all do it and one reason is that we struggle to believe that God's got it under control. So, what do we have to do? Make the choice not to let that happen. His guarantee depends on it.

🌲 Look at this _'Don't Let'_ promise:

🧭 **Philippians 4:6&7** → _Don't let yourself be worried, or troubled, or fearful about anything. Instead, pray about it, telling God what you need. Then, (with faith), thank him for what he's done and is going to do. If you do this, God's peace, which is beyond full understanding, will guard your thoughts from worry and your hearts from being troubled or afraid, all while you live your life united with Christ._

Did you notice that it says not to worry about..._anything_? That doesn't leave room for us to be selective about what we choose to worry about, does it?

And you already get the idea about those two words - _"Don't let"_, right? It's a _choice_ we make not to allow ourselves to worry. The choice is totally ours. The idea here is to replace the worry with prayer. Instead of telling others what we're worried about, tell God. Tell him what you need from him. Then, thank him for what he's going to do and experience his peace. He's got it under control. **Do you believe that?**

Did you notice in that verse it says that God's peace is <u>beyond</u> <u>our understanding</u>? That tells us that his peace is so different from the world's peace, we should be able to *feel* the difference. It should *feel* distinct and unique from any peace we've known living in this world.

And don't miss the last part of that promise. It says God's peace will <u>*guard*</u> our thoughts and our emotions. → That word in the Greek means <u>to protect from *hostile invasion*</u>. That's important. The enemy of our souls wants to invade our thoughts and our hearts so he can lead us down the path of worry, anxious thoughts, doubt, and fear.
Do you wanna know the cool part, though? → God promises to use *his peace* to <u>guard</u> our minds and our hearts from invasion by the enemy. That means the enemy can't get through. Worry and fear are kept away. They won't affect us. **But that won't happen until** we *'let go'* of our worries, turn to God, letting him know our concerns and trusting him to take care of it all. Then *his* peace will flow. It's kind of a promise with a <u>condition</u> to it.

The bottom-line is this → It really comes down to <u>a choice</u>:
A <u>choice</u> to not let ourselves be worried... a <u>choice</u> to take it to God...a <u>choice</u> to release the situation into his hands...and a <u>choice</u> to trust him to do what he thinks is best (regardless of what we want), and of course, a <u>choice</u> to <u>let</u> *his* peace fill us.
And, if we start to take the worry back again...that's when we need to hand it back over to God, over and over again until it becomes less ours and more God's. Try it for yourself and see what happens. <u>That's how we grow our faith</u>.

🌲**Now that we have that <u>gift of peace</u> that Jesus gave us, what do we do with it? Here's a *'<u>Let</u>'* verse:**

✦ <u>Colossians 3:15</u> → <u>*Let*</u> *(allow) the peace that Christ gives you <u>rule</u> and reign over your thoughts and emotions.*

Do you see that word *'<u>let</u>'*? That means it's up to us to <u>*allow*</u> it to happen...to *let* Jesus's peace have supreme sovereign reign over all our troubled thoughts. **It means** his peace gets to rule our hearts, it gets to have the last say...not worry or fear. God won't do that part for us. It's up to us. Yup...it's a choice.

You might be thinking → *"Well I try but I can't help it. I keep going back to what's troubling me."*

I get it, we all do it, but just know this → God's well aware of your struggles and so he gives you *his* strength to handle it. **Look at this next guarantee:**

Colossians 1:11 (the 111 verse) → *God will strengthen you with his own power,* (so that you will have his strength within you, and his strength becomes your strength). *Then, when trouble comes your way, you won't give up, but instead, you'll have all the patience and endurance you need to handle the situation.*

The key to that verse is right there. Do you see it? God will give us *his* strength, and *his* strength becomes our strength. There's an old saying→ *"Give God your weakness and he'll give you his strength."* It sounds simple...and it is...sort of. All we need to do is believe it, trust him for it, and receive it.
Believe – Trust – Receive. → It's a *choice* we need to make.

You might be thinking → *"Well, that's easy for you to say. I try to believe and trust God, but I struggle with it."*.

I'm right there with you. I wrestle with believing and trusting God, just like we all do. But just remember, you can't lose faith if you don't have any faith. So, if you're struggling with faith, that means you've got faith. You just need to grow it. So, think about it; that leaves us two choices: → let God grow our faith *or* not. It comes down to a **choice**. Choices, choices, choices. It's always a choice, isn't it? Are you tired of me saying it yet?☺

By the way, what is it exactly that God is strengthening in us? Have you ever thought about that? I'll tell you what I think. When he gives us *his* strength, I think it's physical strength, or it's emotional strength, or it's spiritual strength. It's different for each of us. **God knows exactly the type of strength we need:** → Are you feeling worn out and tired from the stress and worry? **His strength in you** will make you physically stronger.

→ Are you <u>mentally and emotionally drained</u>? **His strength in you** will help you to handle the things you're going through.
→ Are you <u>spiritually dry and empty</u>? **His strength in you** will build your faith so you can keep on going.
Got it? → It's his strength in you.

<u>**You may ask**</u> → *"Well, how can you be so sure of that?"*

My answer is that Jesus and the apostle Paul (the authors of those last two verses) are either telling the truth or they're lying to us. Which one do you think it is?

You know what? Maybe some of us need to get beyond doubt and get into believing God for what he says he'll do for us. <u>After all, is believing really any harder than doubting</u>?

Someone once said: *"Feed your faith and starve your doubt."* That's a good place to start. I think some of us might look a little spiritually gaunt these days because we're feeding our doubt and starving our faith. So, why don't we do the opposite? Let's feed on what God says in his Word...then believe it and confess it in our hearts...continually. That's what it means to feed our faith and starve our doubts. Plus, it <u>honors God</u> when we do.

Just remember this: To God, <u>trusting him</u> is really important. I mean, it's a REALLY big deal to him. He makes that clear all through the Bible. The fact is, he's greatly honored when we trust in what he says he'll do us, rather than doubt him.

But there's more to it than that. God knows that trusting him will help us by taking our eyes off our problems. It helps us bring God into the center of every situation. And that keeps God in the center of our lives. That's where he wants to live.

Just look at the Israelites when they were in the desert, heading to the Promise Land. God was right there with them. Yet they weren't allowed to enter the land God wanted to give them, nor enjoy the blessings of the life God had waiting for them. Why? Because they dishonored God by <u>not trusting him</u> when things got hard. He was ready to give them a land of abundance. He guaranteed it, and if they had just trusted in what he said he would do for them, they would've had a great life...not wandering around in a hot, desolate desert for years on end. In fact, all through the Bible, you can read about amazing things God did for people...all because they trusted him and did what he told them to do. So, let's avoid this *blessing-blocker*. Let's trust him and enter into his abundant life of blessings.

You know what I think we need to practice? → Our A,B,C's
A- **Agree** with God in what he says he wants to do for us.
B- **Believe** it will actually happen...believe his guarantees.
C- **Confess** it continually to feed our faith and starve our doubts. You're never a loser unless you lose faith in God.

Would you like to live in complete and total peace *all* **the time? Then, look at this *'let'* promise:**

Isaiah 26:3 → *God will continually keep in complete and total peace all those who **let** their trust be solely in him* (who totally rely on him and are completely confident in his wisdom and his ways, his abilities, and his power, thus no worries or fears). *And he will keep in total peace all those who **let** their thoughts be fixed on him* (instead of their worries or their fears).

There are two things to see here.
1.) What God says he will do.
2.) What God says we should do.

He'll do the *keeping-us-in-peace* part *(if)* we do the *trusting-in-him* part, and the *fixing-our-thoughts-on-him* part.

It's kind of amazing how simple it is, don't you think? → Put our trust in him, and fix our thoughts on him throughout the day – not our worries, not our anxieties, and not our fears. That's it! And as a result, we can enjoy peace all day long.

Notice that it's *"complete and total peace"* that God's giving. It's not partial peace, or a bit of peace with some worry mixed in. No, it's an all-or-nothing-full-meal-deal → Total Peace

You know what Ernest Hemingway once said? *"The best way to find out if you can trust somebody is to trust them."*
For many of us it's really hard to relinquish control and just blindly *trust* God. But, I'll tell you what, I think good ole Ernest

was right. The best way to find out if we really can trust God is to just go all in and trust him. After all, there's nothing to lose... but *doubt* itself.

Big secret with this next guarantee...Don't miss it:

This is a <u>hidden gem</u>. If you were reading this next verse in the Bible, you might easily pass right by it. **Look at this '<u>*Let*</u>' verse:**

<u>Romans 15:13</u> → *God, the true source of **hope**, will <u>fill</u> you* (Greek meaning – to fill completely to the brim) *with joy and <u>peace</u> *because* you **<u>let</u>** your <u>trust</u> be in him* (not in anything else). *Then, you will <u>overflow </u>with confident hope through the power of the Holy Spirit.*

This is one of the promises I would choose to help me walk through life. The secret to walking around all day with peace and joy and confident hope flowing in our lives, no matter what the circumstance, is found in that guarantee. Do you see it? It's '<u>trusting</u>' God.

WAIT! I know that doesn't sound very exciting but hear me out. If you spent your whole day putting most of your situations into the hands of God, completely *trusting* him with them, what will naturally flow from that process? Yup- *peace* and *joy*...no matter what the circumstances may be.

Let me say it a different way. If you *release*, I mean really <u>let go</u> of controlling the situations in your day and just give them, one by one, over to God, <u>the peace of God</u> will fill you <u>to the brim</u>. That's how Jesus did it. He *'let go and let God'*, in every situation, all day long, every day he lived on earth.

Just try it for one day and see how you feel. It just takes a few seconds for each situation, whether great or small. You start with words and the rest takes place in your heart (the trusting). I'm telling you, if we would <u>practice</u> this daily, we would be walking around inwardly content and free from all our worries, concerns, troubling thoughts, and fears, knowing God's got it covered. We would have a confidence we haven't had before. It takes practice, though. Trust me, I learned it the hard way. But, once you get used to it, it gets easier...then a little easier still. Just remember, you have nothing to gain by doing nothing.☺

Remember this...It's important.
When we honestly and truly entrust to God our circumstances, it *releases* him to operate the way *he* wants, instead of the way we want. And, since God is the author of peace and joy, when he is free to manage our life (because we've released our control) the natural flow from that process will be peace and joy and a confident hope. Ponder that thought. Don't let it go until you've digested it. Then try it for a day. See what happens.

<u>**In that verse we just covered:**</u>
→ **Notice** *where* the <u>peace</u> is coming from— God, no other source but God (not medication, food, marijuana, alcohol, therapy, or intimate relationships...you get the idea)☺
→ **Notice** *what* he'll do with that peace – fill us up to the <u>brim</u> with it. That leaves no room for other stuff like worry and fear.
→ **Notice** what we have to do – *trust* him...really and truly trust him, which like I mentioned, keeps God in the center of our lives and keeps our eyes on him, not our problems.
→ **Notice**, <u>peace,</u> <u>joy,</u> and <u>hope</u> will be the result.

And one more point about that promise:
Again, the Greek meaning of the word *"<u>fill</u>"* is 'to fill to the brim', right? But, what is God filling us to the brim with? → peace and joy and confident hope...*<u>when</u>* we truly and consistently put our trust in him. We don't have to struggle to get this peace, joy, and hope. <u>Our job</u> is to trust God to give them to us. <u>His job</u> is to fill us to the brim with them. Just don't let any *blessing-blockers* interfere with the process.

And think about this → *'to the brim'* means there's absolutely <u>no room left</u> for worry, anxiety, troubled thoughts, fears, or sorrow. None. That's fantastic, isn't it? We can walk through each day absolutely free from those things. Grasp this truth and it will significantly change your life.

The bottom-line is this: A person who is *<u>filled to the brim</u>'* with God's peace, and joy, and as a result, overflows with a confident hope (all because they're letting go of control and completely trusting God to handle things in their life), that person is *not* one who is worried or troubled or fearful. Right? So...let's become one of those people. Let's do our part, and then wait expectantly for God to do his part. After all, he guarantees it. What do we have to lose...but our worries and fears.

How would you like to have God's peace *(not the world's peace)* **in *every* situation in your life?**

2 Thessalonians 3:16 → *May, God, the author of peace, himself give you his peace, at all times, and in every situation.*

God doesn't want us in turmoil. He originally designed our bodies to function in a state of peace and joy at all times. Think about that for a moment. It's healthy for us to always be mentally, physically, and spiritually at peace. Wouldn't you agree? Anything other than that is against God's original design.

→ Who's giving the peace? - God is
→ Who's peace are we getting? - God's
→ How often? – at all times, and in every situation
→ What do we have to do to receive his peace? – Believe it

This verse actually starts off as a prayer. The thing is, the apostle Paul, who wrote it, would not have made this statement if he didn't believe God would do it for us. So, we need to believe it as well.

And get this: At *all times* literally means...at *all* times. *In every situation* means...in *every* situation. You get the point. So, it might be useful for us to check and see *if* we truly are at peace in the situations we're in. If we're missing that peace, then we need to figure out why we're missing it and get that peace back again. Right?

You might be thinking → *"Are you kidding me? That doesn't make any sense. How am I supposed to feel at peace when I've been really hurt by someone...or...when I'm going through a horrendous trial?"*

Good point. My suggestion is to go back to the very beginning of this section and read the quote. It really is all about having Jesus with us in the boat during the storms, don't you think?

And lucky for us, God placed the Holy Spirit in us so we would have him with us in all those terrible situations...to comfort and support us, to strengthen us, to help us, and to counsel us.

Could it be that simple? The irony is, God makes his way of living simple – it's us who seem to make it hard.

Put this in your backpack for your journey through life:

So far, we've seen promises that tell us:
1.) Christ gives us the gift of his peace, and it's different from the peace the world gives. It's up to us to receive it and not let our hearts be troubled. So, do that. MAC it = **M**ake **A C**hoice

2.) We need to let the peace that comes from Christ reign over and govern our thoughts and emotions, so they don't get out of control and start to cause us problems. Do that as well.

3.) God says he'll keep us in a state of complete peace...*if* we trust him and fix our thoughts on him throughout the day. It would be wise to do that also.

4.) God says he'll give us his peace at all times and in every situation. He said it, so believe it and receive it.

I think too many of us walk around acting like we have peace when we really don't. Let's be honest. Too many of us are worried what others may think of us if they knew we were struggling. I say, let's make '*his peace*' real in our lives. Then we won't have to pretend. It's good to be real in front of others anyway. Why are we so afraid to do that? So, **ABC** these things:
Agree with God on what he guarantees about giving you peace.
Believe in your heart that he won't fail to do what he promises.
Confess these promises in your heart or out loud (whichever makes you comfortable), to feed your faith and starve your doubt.

We've got this. We can do it. If we follow those steps, we'll enjoy his peace filling us to the brim. God wants that for us. He wants it for you, even amidst your sad or bad circumstances.

There are two more verses I need to cover, but I really don't want to. People don't like to hear words like '*sin*' or 'control' or 'the flesh', but I think it's necessary if we're going to have God's peace in our lives. Here they are:

✹ **Romans 8:6** → *Letting our old sin-bent nature (the flesh) control our life just leads to spiritual deadness and ruin. But letting the Holy Spirit guide our thoughts and actions will lead to genuine life and abundant peace.*

There's one thing that can keep us from experiencing the peace that God offers. Trust me, I know what it is because it's kept me from having peace more times than I care to share. What's the roadblock? – The *'flesh'*.

What is the 'flesh'? → It's the part of us that functions apart from God's influence. It's the part of us that wants our own way. It's 'self'...the root of the phrase 'self-centered'...the root of the word 'selfishness'. It's my nickname...at least that's what I've been told at times☺.

But, here's the thing → Don't let your *'flesh'* become a roadblock. Let God's Spirit direct your life instead of your *'flesh'* controlling the show. Then, according to this verse, peace will be a result.

After reading that guarantee/promise we just covered, how do we know if the Holy Spirit is truly directing our life?
Answer→ **By our fruit.**

✹ **Galatians 5:22** → *The Holy Spirit produces this kind of fruit in our lives* (when we are submitted to his authority, direction, and guidance): *love for others, joy, peace, patience, kindness, genuine goodness, faithfulness, gentleness, and self-control.*

Did you catch it? 'Peace' is one of the fruit that should be growing on our branches. And what can keep *peace* from becoming one of these fruits in our lives? → Yup...the *'flesh'*.

Here's an easy solution for dealing with our *'flesh'*. Ready for it?

✹ **Jeremiah 17:10** → *Search me, God, and know my hidden thoughts. Examine me and know the true motives of my heart. And point out anything that you want to change in me. Then* *help me to go down the right path that leads towards your everlasting life.*

Warning: If you pray words that are similar to that verse and really mean it, you are just asking for it. I mean it, (literally and metaphorically speaking...lol). When I started praying this verse, whew, it was humiliating...and...painful. God showed me stuff I thought I already had a handle on. Man, was I wrong! He put people and circumstances in my life just to bring out my *fleshly* thoughts and behavior. It was embarrassing. He'll do the same for you...so heed my warning...don't pray this verse unless you want to see the ugly stuff that may be hidden within you.

It's not a bad thing, though. It's a good thing. It's what the Bible calls the *'sanctification process'* – It's God pointing out all the not-so-nice stuff he wants to change in us, and then it's us *letting* him deal with it so he can make us more like his Son.
But it's hard dealing with all the ugly parts in us. It's not fun. It can become uncomfortable, especially when we think we have our spiritual act together.

So, guess what? → We have a <u>choice</u>. Yup – there's that word again. We can either *let* God point all that ugly stuff out to us and then *let* him deal with it in us...or...not. But just remember, if we don't cooperate with God and *let* it happen, then all that fleshly behavior just hangs around and gets in the way of us growing up in God and enjoying <u>his peace</u>.

Guarantee: I can give you a guarantee, though. → If you pray that verse out and really mean it from your heart...then God will answer it. If you're really listening and watching for it, he'll point out the fleshly parts of your life for you to see. And if you surrender them to God and let him deal with them in your life, those *'roadblocks'* of the flesh will be removed, and the <u>peace</u> will start flowing like a river through your life. (*'peace like a river'*...get it?...No? It's one of those old hymns people used to sing. Ok, never mind...let's move on to the next verse.)

Another Roadblock:

Isaiah 48:18 God speaking→ *Oh, if you had only paid attention to my instructions and continually obeyed them as I* *told you to, then you would have had <u>peace flowing like a river</u>....*

(Maybe that's where they got that song from☺). Who doesn't want *peace* just meandering like a river through their life? But what did the people in this verse fail to do that kept that peace from flowing? → They weren't paying attention to God, nor were they careful to follow his instructions, and consequently, they <u>lost the peace</u>. That, my friend, is a *roadblock* to peace. Don't let that *blessing-blocker* happen to you.

Just Reverse It → If you reverse the meaning of that verse, it becomes a promise you can cling to:

✔ **If** we <u>pay attention</u> to what God tells us to do.

✔ **If** we're careful to <u>apply his instructions</u> to our lives, and <u>practice</u> them over and over again until they become a habit.

✔**Then** we'll enjoy peace flowing like a river through our hearts and our lives, just as God guarantees.

Here's where the letters **RAP** come in. → **R**ead it...**A**pply it... **P**ractice it...over and over again. **Be a *'rapper'*.** (What! Way too cheesy for you?)

Before we go further, it would be good to explain what the word *'<u>peace</u>'* means. If you were to ask people what they think *peace* means, you'll get all kinds of descriptions. But which one is accurate?

Here's a good definition of *'peace'* derived from the Greek meaning of the word found in the New Testament:
It's the freedom from all worries, freedom from being troubled, freedom from anxieties and fears, freedom from being irritated over things, freedom from inner and outer conflicts.

That pretty much sums it up for me, but when you add it to the Old Testament Hebrew meaning for *'peace'* which is the word "<u>shalom</u>" it kind of rounds it out even more→ 'shalom peace' is *quietness, tranquility, safety, contentment, health, prosperity, with no worries or fears.*

<u>Mix those definitions together</u> and you have an amazing reason to want peace in your life. I mean, who wouldn't want all those good things? Right?

How would you like to have a huge amount of that kind of peace as you walk through life - not just a bit of peace that comes and goes, but a humongous, mammoth, enormous, elephantine, gargantuan amount of peace? Check out this guarantee:

Psalm 119:165 → *Those who have a <u>passion for God's instructions</u> will have a <u>great amount of peace</u>* (meaning - a huge amount of it). *Nothing will cause them to <u>stumble</u> or fall in their walk through life.*

With a guarantee like that, how can we go wrong? Ok, you're right. I forgot. → It can go wrong...really wrong for us. There will be a bunch of stumbling and falling going on as we struggle through life *if* we don't have a desire for his instructions. In fact, the Hebrew word for '*stumble*' literally means '*roadblock*'.

Want to remove the 'roadblocks' in the pathways of your life? Then, develop a passion for God's instructions on how to live your life, and follow through with doing them so you won't stumble. And as a result, get a <u>huge amount of peace</u> added into the mix; not just a small amount...an enormous amount.

Oh, by the way...here's a <u>health tip</u>: Did you know that God promises us that if we have his peace flowing in our life, it helps us sleep at night and it improves our health?

Psalm 4:8 → *As I lay with <u>your peace in my heart</u>, I sleep restfully, knowing that I'm safe, secure, and right with you, God.*

Proverbs 14:30 → *Having a <u>heart at peace</u> leads to a healthy body.*

There are other verses about *'peace'* that we'll cover...but they're in other sections of this book because *peace* is often a consequence of doing other stuff God wants us to do. You'll see.

Put this also in your backpack for your journey in life:

Summary of Steps To His Peace

✅God gives us his peace as a _gift_. So, receive it and enjoy it.

✅We need to _let_ his peace rule over our thoughts and emotions, so things don't get out of hand, and we end up blowing it.

✅God will _keep us in total peace_ when we completely _trust_ Him and _fix_ our thoughts on him throughout our day.

✅When we _give_ our worries and concerns to God in prayer and _thank_ him with faith and expectation for the answers, we'll have _his_ peace and _his_ peace will _protect_ our thoughts and emotions from worry and fear.

✅When we _let_ God's Holy Spirit rule over our thoughts, emotions, and actions, instead of the flesh doing so, it will bring us abundant life and abundant peace.

✅When we develop a _passion_ for God's Word and are careful to _do_ what it says, we can expect a huge amount of peace to flow through our lives.

No God, no peace
Know God, know peace
Croft Pentz

WORRY
How to Become Worry-Free

Do you ever get tired from worry? Medically speaking, we know it can negatively affect our health.

I like what Corrie Ten Boom once wrote: *"Worry doesn't empty tomorrow of its sorrow. It empties today of its strength."*

Did you know God is adamantly against worry?

Jesus, Paul, and the apostles, as well as several Old Testament writers all spoke against it.

I think most of us worry without realizing we're just filling in the gap of not trusting God. We treat it like it's an option, that we're free to worry if we choose to. But it's not an option. Nowhere in God's Word does it encourage us to worry.

People think they have a lot to worry about in their lives, but you know what Mark Twain once said. "*I have known a great many troubles, but most of them never happened.*"
That leaves a lot of wasted time worrying, doesn't it?

So, what are we supposed to do?

Psalm 55:22 → *Give* to God (meaning, release into his hands and let go of) *all of your worries and burdens* (those things that weigh you down). *If you do this, he'll take good care of you* (meaning, he'll hold you up, sustain you, so you'll make it through). *In fact, he will never allow his righteous ones to be shaken* (slip or fall flat on their faces).

This is what God guarantees he will do for you:

1.) He'll take <u>good care of you</u> and <u>hold you up</u> you so you can make it through the tough times. It's in his heart to do so.

It's important not to pass by the meaning of that phrase. In the Hebrew language, it means God will personally wrap his arms around you and hold you close; that he'll nourish and encourage you, so you'll be able to continue. That's what he guarantees.

2.) He won't let you fall flat on your face. You're not going to fail...unless *you* let it happen. That's what he guarantees.

✅ What does God expect you to do?

1.) <u>Let go of</u> (completely release) your worries and burdens by putting them into God's hands. That means don't take them back. God's got em, so let him keep em. It's a choice we make.

2.) <u>Make sure</u> you're one of the *'righteous ones'* mentioned in that verse. How? By continually doing the things he tells you to do in his Word. That's what *'righteous'* means – you're consistently doing what is *right*).

By the way, *'letting go'* in that verse means completely releasing our grip on our worries. If we've done that, then our hands should be *empty* and the weight on our shoulders should be lifted, right? I mean, we should feel lighter, happier, and at peace. We should sleep better because we've let go of all our worries. So, check yourself. Have you truly *'let go'*?

Just remember that God won't take our worry away for us. We have to *give it to him*. Faith is putting all your eggs in God's basket. That means your basket of worries should be <u>empty</u>.

I'll tell you what often happens instead: Believe me, I know this from my own struggles in learning this principle. We might wake up the next morning feeling pretty tired and worn out. Why is that? It's because we really haven't *totally* given our worries to God. We may think we've done it...but we really haven't. We've taken some of it back again and they've just been stewing inside us all night long. So, we wake up exhausted.

You know what? God totally understands this because he made us. He smiles at us. He doesn't frown with disapproval, or lose his patience with us, or get upset because we keep taking our worries back. He wants us to be free of stress. He didn't design us to live with stress in our bodies. He doesn't want us to carry those burdens all by ourselves. He comes alongside us and holds out his hands, just waiting for us to give those worries back to him. That's our God. Yeah, I know, I'll say it again – He's always good to us...*all* of the time...not just some of the time...*all* of the time. Wouldn't you agree?

So, when the enemy starts to plant those thoughts of worry in your head, just tell him to back off and go talk to God...he's the one holding your worries, not you.

Remember this as well → Faith is developed by focusing on God's truth. Worry is developed by focusing on the enemy's lies. So, feed your faith and starve your worries...focus on what God says is the truth and deny the lie.

Arthur Roche once wrote: *"Worry is a thin stream of fear trickling through the mind. If allowed to continue, it cuts a deep channel into which all other thoughts are drained."*

Don't let that happen to you. Don't hold onto your worries that they consume you. Get rid of them quickly. Just give them back to God again...and again...and again. And just do what God tells us to do in this next verse:

Psalm 46:10 → *Be* still (Hebrew meaning – sink down and relax, just let it go) *and* learn *to know that I am God.*

In this society, we're not used to being *still*. We look for something to distract us, to keep us occupied...like our phones, or social media, music or TV. Learning to be still before God is not easy, but it's necessary if we're going to become worry-free.

That phrase *"learn to know that I am God"* in the Hebrew language implies it's a *learning* process. It takes time. So, don't be hard on yourself. But notice that in order to know that God is God, we need to slow down and be still before him. If we would do that then we'd hear from God more often, trust him more, and we'd become more certain of who he is.

Bear this in mind: Our worried thoughts have to be replaced by something else. If we've been focused on our worries, why not focus on God's promises instead...like this next guarantee:

✦ **LUKE 12:7** Jesus speaking → *Listen, God even knows the number of hairs on your head. So, <u>don't let</u> yourself be worried or afraid. You're more valuable to God than anything else in all his creation.*

That phrase *'<u>Don't let yourself be worried or afraid</u>'* is mentioned in the Bible 365 times in various ways. That's like one for every day of the year, isn't it? Huh. I guess there's not a single day we have to be worried. Right?☺

Why would God bother to count the number of hairs on your head, which is something pretty insignificant to do if you think about it. It's because he's making a point here.→ You matter so much to him, that he pays attention to the little stuff as well as the big stuff going on in your life. After all, if he didn't care, he wouldn't bother to count your hair. Right?

So, if you're thinking that God seems really far away, or he doesn't seem to care about what's going on in your life, then just review that promise we just covered. God wants you to understand that *if* he knows the ever-changing numbers of hairs on your head, then he's *also* paying attention to the bigger things in your life as well...like your problems.

If you don't believe this, then it will be really hard to trust him with your worries.

And remember, that verse is a <u>promise</u>: Notice 3 things
1.) God guarantees to <u>notice</u> all of the details of our lives, from the number of hairs all the way up to the bigger, more important stuff.

2.) God promises us that he considers us to be <u>more valuable</u> than anything else in the universe....let me say it again – more than anything else in the whole universe. So, take a chance and believe that he notices you and all of the intricacies of what's going on in your circumstances. <u>Just make sure</u> you invite him into the middle of your life. If you keep him at a distance...then that's what you'll get.

3.) Jesus tells us to <u>not allow</u> ourselves to worry or be afraid. How do we do that? By doing what he told us to do...<u>make a</u>

choice. It's a choice we make to *not let* ourselves fall into the trap of worrying.

People say to me, *"I'm addicted to worry. I can't stop myself from worrying."* What??? Yes, you can. It's a *choice* you make. It's not an addiction. It's like that old saying→ *Those who think they can't, won't. Those who believe they can, will.*

You know what I'm going to recommend, don't you? Just **ABC** it.

✅**Agree** with what God's saying in that last verse – that he knows the exact amount of hair on your head and that you're more valuable to him than all the rest of his creation.

✅**Believe** and be convinced in your heart that *if* he knows the number of hairs on your head, then he certainly knows exactly what you're going through and all the details of your situation.

✅**Confess** it (whether out loud or in your heart) over and over again to feed your faith and starve your worry.

What would that sound like? → Something like this: *"God you say that I'm so valuable to you that you know the number of hairs on my head, and if you know that, then you also know the details of the situation I'm going through. So, I choose not to worry. I put my situation into your hands, and since you've got my life in your hands, I'll just trust you instead of worrying..."*

Ok, I have to admit, it does seem a bit hard to believe that God actually knows the number of hairs on our heads at any given time. After all, we lose hair and grow new ones continually. It seems a bit far-fetched...until...we realize who it was that made that statement in that verse. It was Jesus, who claimed he came from God's home and knew him intimately. Sooooo, either he was lying when he said it...or...he was telling us the truth based on his inside knowledge of God. I'll leave that up to you.

While you're deciding about that, think about this→ How hard is it for God to count the hairs on our heads? I mean, if he's capable of creating millions of galaxies so big and suns so much larger than our own that we can't even wrap our heads around it, then I'm guessing that knowing how many hairs we own on our head is pretty easy for him. Wouldn't you agree? So, what are we worried about? God knows exactly what's going on in our lives.

Again, if you don't feel God cares very much about you, then read this promise:

Mathew 10:29,31 Jesus speaking → *What is the value of a bird? It costs practically nothing. Yet not one bird falls dead to the ground without God personally knowing and caring about it. So, don't allow yourself to worry. After all, you're much more valuable to God than even a flock of thousands of birds.*

Now, read this guarantee:

Mathew 6:30-34 Jesus speaking→ *I want you to understand this, if God takes such good care of the beautiful wildflowers in the field, which are simply here today and gone tomorrow, then he will most certainly take good care of you. So, why then do you have such small faith and so little trust in God?*

All three of those verses we just covered were spoken by Jesus. And not just that, all three of those verses have the same implication.→ If God takes such an interest in the numbers of hairs on our heads, and if he cares so much about each bird that dies when no one's around, and if he takes such good care of the wildflowers in fields that are far away from the human eye, then he guarantees to notice and take an interest in our worries and our struggles. He's ready and willing to help us.
The question is, if Jesus said it, do you believe it? Because, if you believe it, then your worries will have to flee from you.

It's also interesting that Jesus marveled at why his listeners had such little faith in trusting God to personally provide for them. Didn't they know they were way more important to God than birds and flowers? It's the same kind of faith and trust Jesus had in God when he was on the Sea of Galilee, fast asleep in a boat, totally at peace, with no worry...right in the middle of a raging storm with waves that threatened to sink the vessel. (See Mark 4:35). He expects us to have the same kind of trust.

The passage continues:

✦ **Verse 31** Jesus speaking→ *So, don't allow yourselves to be worried about these things, saying, "How are we going to make it?" These worries dominate the minds of underbelievers. But your father in heaven **already** knows **all** of your needs.*

You know what Jesus is saying here? → Unbelievers worry, but believers don't. Why would they if God already knows all their needs? The only thing that really stands between worry and no worries...is doubt. Where do you stand?

It's been said that fear ends where faith begins. It really does come down to Faith over Fear.

FAITH = **F**ull **A**ssurance **I**n **T**he **H**eart
Until we have that full assurance resting in our hearts – that God deeply cares about us, that he knows what we're going through, and that he's fully invested in helping us...until we believe that fact with certainty, fear and worry will occupy our hearts instead.

So, what are we going to do with this passage we just covered?
- **MAC** it, meaning, we're going to **M**ake **A** **C**hoice. To do what? → To trust God and not worry.
- **ABC** it, meaning we're going to **A**gree with God that he *already* knows *all* our needs and will take care of us. We're going to **B**elieve it enough until the worries disappear...And then, we going to **C**onfess it over and over again to feed our faith and keep the worries away.
  Oh man, I just can't stop with the acronyms. ☺

The passage continues: Here's the important part.

✦ **Verse 33** Jesus speaking→ *So, instead of worrying, focus your attention on seeking God's kingdom above everything else in your life, and seek the right way to live that he prescribes. Do this and all the other things you need and strive for will be provided.*

This is a promise where we need to do a heart check and ask ourselves. → *"Am I doing those things? Am I seeking God's kingdom first in my life, above everything else that interests me? And am I paying attention and being careful to walk in God's* *ways? Or, could it be that the daily grind and the distractions of life are consuming me and keeping me from doing it?"*

It doesn't mean we have to spend every waking hour seeking his kingdom. It means it must be a top priority in where our interests lie. It should be the main focus in our lives. Jesus wouldn't have repeatedly mentioned the importance of seeking God's kingdom if it weren't important. Right?

<u>**You might be thinking**</u> → *"I don't get it. What does it even mean to 'seek his kingdom'?"*

You're not alone. When I've asked believers how they personally seek God's kingdom, many of them fumble for words. They aren't sure. **So, let me make this short and sweet:** The Greek meaning for the word "**<u>seek first</u>**", in the verse we're talking about is this → To crave something so badly that nothing's going to get in the way of you seeking it. And until you find it, you just won't be satisfied. That's what's meant by *'seeking God's kingdom first'* in our lives.

Look at it this way: Whatever we spend the majority of our time, our interests, and our efforts on, that's what we're ultimately seeking after. How about you? Again, you may need to do a heart-check with real honesty to figure this one out. I have to do it constantly in my own life. I can easily get distracted. So, we need to get this one right. It's critical.

<u>**You might be thinking**</u> → *"I don't get it. What exactly is 'God's kingdom', anyway?"*

Glad you asked. → The kingdom of God, according to the Bible, is simply the realm in heaven and on earth where God reigns and his will is done. As his kids, we're supposed to be living in that kingdom. Of course, there's more to it than that, but that's a foundation point on which all the rest is built.

Every kingdom has a king, and the king that God appointed for his kingdom is his anointed one, the risen Christ. Jesus has been *'appointed and anointed'* to be our king. (Sorry, I just liked the way that sounded.☺). And any king has loyal subjects...us.

So, we need to decide:

Who's on the throne in our life – God or us? After all, if we're going to seek God's kingdom, then ultimately he has to be the king...not us. And if he's king in our lives, then our allegiance must go to what pleases him, not just what pleases us.

Luckily for us, we don't have to figure out what he wants. It's all written out for us. Just seek out and follow the King's instructions in his Word. Do that and you can't go wrong.

One other thing about 'seeking his kingdom':

God's kingdom is filled to the brim with blessings and good things. It's a fun place to be. When we seek his kingdom, it's ok to seek those blessings and good things as well. God had us in mind when he made them. They would be wasted if we didn't receive them. In his kingdom, it's all good → prosperity, success, friendships, wisdom, protection, healing, joy, laughter, fun, peace, happiness, etc. **It's all for his loyal subjects – us.**

<u>**Put this in your backpack in your walk through life**</u>:

If you want to stop worrying about stuff in your life, then do these 4 steps:

SEEK = <u>S</u>eek + <u>E</u>lect + <u>E</u>xpect + <u>K</u>eep

1. **<u>Seek</u>** his kingship. Take your mind <u>off</u> your worries and put it on seeking God's kingdom and the good things he offers his kids.

2. **<u>Elect</u>** him to be king in your life and take yourself 'off' the throne. Remember, '*Lord*' means we serve him, not us.

3. **<u>Expect</u>** all the other things you've been striving for and worried about to be provided and worked out by your king.

4. **<u>Keep</u>** the king's edicts (living the way he tells us to in his Word) so he can keep you safe and bless you with good things.

By the way, that verse above is a powerful <u>promise</u> to **ABCD** & '**<u>E</u>**'. Yeah, another letter. The "<u>E</u>" stands for "<u>Expect</u>" → Expecting God to come through with what he says he'll do. No doubts allowed. It'll feed your faith. So, <u>expect</u> good things.

Don't worry...we're not going to cover the whole alphabet ☺.

<u>Agree</u> with God that he's king and you're not and that his kingdom is worth seeking above all else in your life.

<u>Believe</u> that God really will provide for you, just as he said he would.

Confess these things over and over again to feed your faith and starve your worry if it tries to creep back.

Do what's necessary to make God your king, seeking his kingdom first, and the way of living he prescribes. Just do it! (Hey, isn't there a slogan….?)

Expect to see God provide all your needs, just as he said he would. Expecting something involves waiting for it. Be patient.

Remember: God always wants the very best for you. He doesn't want you to worry about anything at all. Imagine living life free of all worry. – Jesus did.

Here's the final verse of that passage:

✦ Verse 34 Jesus speaking→ *So, just don't worry about what's going to happen tomorrow or the days thereafter. Each day brings enough troubles of its own.*

When you think about it, worrying is moving into tomorrow ahead of time. It's carrying tomorrow's load with today's strength – and that's carrying two days at once. That can be exhausting.

I like what Dale Carnegie said: "Today is the tomorrow you worried about yesterday." Isn't that the truth!!!

Notice that Jesus says in that verse that each day will bring its own set of troubles. It's a fact of life. The question is...does that mean we need to worry about them? Nope, because God has specific things he tells us to do with all the troubles that come our way...and *worry* isn't one of them.

🌲 Here are 3 reminder-verses that we've already covered in other sections: If you *ABCD & E* these promises, you'll have powerful weapons to use against worry.

✦ 1 Peter 5:7 → *Cast (throw) all your worries and concerns onto God* (release them into God's hands and let go), *because he cares about you with deep affection.*

✦ **Psalm 37:5** → _Commit_ everything you're doing to the Lord. (Hebrew meaning – roll each one of your cares, your worries, and concerns in each situation, onto God's shoulders). _Trust him with them all_ (with bold confidence) _and he will help you_ (Hebrew meaning - He will work it all out for you. He will attend to it and put it all in order).

✦ **Psalm 55:22** → _Give_ to God (release out of your hands and put into God's hands) all your worries and burdens (those things that weigh you down). _Do this and he will take care of you and hold you together_ (he'll sustain you so you can keep going).

3 things you can take from those verses:
1. Throw or roll those worries and concerns onto God and only him. Release them out of your hands and don't take them back.
2. Entrust them to him (let go...and let God).
3. He'll take good care of you and he'll work it all out for you. You can stop trying to fix it and just rest, knowing God's got it.

Wanna know your main weapon against worry? TRUST.
I would recommend that you read the section in this book on Trust. There are verses there that will also help in dealing with worry.

TRUST God→ How to use it against worry:
T = Take your worries to the Lord in prayer.
R = Review his guarantees on trust and worry.
U = Utter in your heart or out loud those guarantees.
S = Surrender your situations to God and the outcome he wants.
T = Train yourself to do this over and over again.

🌲One more guarantee I want to review with you:

✦ **Philippians 4:6&7** →_Don't let_ yourself be worried, troubled, or afraid about one single thing. Instead, pray about it, telling God what you need. Then, (with faith), thank him for what he's done and is going to do. If you do this, _God's own peace_, which is way beyond our understanding, will _keep_ (guard) your thoughts from worry and your hearts from being troubled or afraid; all of this as you live your life united with Christ Jesus.

✅**What does God expect us to do with our worry and troubling thoughts?**

1.) Take them to him in prayer. Release them into his hands, giving God *all* our worries...letting go and letting God.

2.) Thank him in advance for what he's going to do to help us.

✅**What does God guarantee us?**

1.) He'll give us *his* peace which is different from any other peace we've ever known. That peace will only come because he's taking care of things for us, whether the outcome is to our liking or not. We can rest. He's got it covered.

2.) His peace will *keep* our thoughts away from worry and our emotions from being upset and stressed out.

That word "*keep*" in that verse we just covered, in the Greek, means to be like a Roman sentry who stands ready to prevent a hostile invasion.

Think about that for a moment. God is saying he'll protect our thoughts and emotions from a hostile invasion by the evil-one. *If* we do our part, then God will keep those worries, troubled thoughts, and fears far away from us. That's an amazing promise! Only our pride would say, "I've got this covered.", but surrender says, "God's got me covered."

Don't miss the significance of *thanking him*, in that verse. For What? For what he's *going* to do. Can you see you're exercising your faith when you're thanking him? You're expressing your *confidence* to God that he'll help you, even if you haven't seen it yet. After all, if you were doubting whether God would help you, then you wouldn't be thanking him for what he's *going* to do. Right? Sort of a tongue-twister there, but you get the idea.

Remember this: Prayer is bringing our cares and worries to God. Faith is leaving them there.

And get this: According to medical research, when we're holding onto a lot of worry, it gets stored in our cells throughout our bodies in the form of a continual *stress-response*. As a result, we can exhaust our immune system which is responsible for helping us deal with stress in our lives. When the immune system becomes overworked and exhausted it can't protect us very well from sickness or disease. That's a vicious cycle isn't it?

Plus, according to medical science, sustained long-term worry over months or even years seems to change the composition of our blood – I'm talking about components such as *homocysteine*, which is linked to heart disease, or *interleukin3*, a cytokine that can diminish immune efficiency and cause inflammation throughout our bodies, or excess *cortisol*, which has ties to high blood sugar levels. In fact, sustained worry has ties to problems with kidneys, digestion, immune function, strokes, ulcers…the list goes on.

Remember this: God didn't design us to have worries, let alone, hold onto to them. He knew what it would do to our bodies. It was never part of his original creation. So, let go of your worry.

Bottom-line: Stop worrying about what can go wrong and get excited about what can go right. Got it?

TROUBLE
How God Promises To Help

Winston Churchill once said: *"If you're going through hell, keep going."* I love that. That just speaks to us in our daily lives, doesn't it?

There are people on this earth that are wonderful followers of God, who live good and godly lives. Yet, they experience tragedies and calamities and troubles they didn't ask for.
So, why is that?

It's not so easy to answer, but **one main reason is** that God isn't the only one at work in this world. You might recall Jesus saying we have an enemy who wants to steal from us, destroy us, and crush all that is good in our lives (See John 10:10). And perhaps you've heard the apostle Peter's warning that the evil-one is like a roaring lion, prowling about, searching for those he can destroy (See 1 Peter 5:8).
As weird as it seems, there is a battle always going on between light and darkness, good and evil, and because of this, guess what?...Bad things will happen to good people.

You know what? God's Word does not say that we won't have trouble in our lives. It does repeatedly say, however, that God will *always* help us through our trouble and even rescue us from it. Here's what he guarantees:

Psalm 46:1→ *God is <u>always</u> ready to help us in times of trouble or distress.*

And how about this promise:

✦ **Hebrew 4:16** → *Let's approach the very* <u>throne of God</u> *with confidence. There we'll receive his favor, and his goodwill, and his kindness, to help us in our time of trouble.*

Did you know that one of the privileges we have as God's children is the birth-right to come into his throne-room <u>anytime</u> we want help from God. That's amazing when you think about it. We can walk right up to the very throne of the creator of the universe and get his help, and we can be sure of a happy welcome.

Here's the thing, though. Even though that's exactly what that verse says, many of us struggle to believe it, and I certainly understand why. After all, God can often seem far away at times, so it's kind of hard to imagine stepping right before his throne. But the irony is, if we don't believe it, then we flat-out rob ourselves of an amazing guarantee of help.

People think such a thought is sacrilegious → *"I can't just walk right up to God's throne. That's just not right!"*

And so, they stand outside his throne room, wishing God would do something. The thing they have to grasp is that he invites us in (See Hebrews 10:19). The curtain in the temple that once separated a holy God from sinful humanity was torn from top to bottom. God made himself accessible to us once again (See Mathew 27:51). So, if we're his adopted, forgiven children, and we've been invited into his presence, then all we need is the faith to <u>approach</u> him with confidence (See Ephesians 3:12).

<u>**You might be saying to yourself**</u> → *"That just seems hard to believe. I don't even know how to enter this 'throne-room' you're talking about."*

Guess what? You're already there! Through Christ, you belong in the very throne-room of God. You're sitting <u>with him</u> in heaven right now. Say whaaat??? I get what you're thinking. It's crazy!!! But I didn't make this stuff up. God says it in his Word. Look at what he says:

✦ **Ephesians 2:6** → *Because we're united with Christ, God raised us from eternal death* <u>together</u> *with Christ when he was* *resurrected, and he <u>seated us together with him</u> in the heavenly realm.*

<u>**What's Christ seated on?**</u> A throne…in the heavenly realm, in the highest place of honor, at the right hand of God (See Ephesians 1:20). So, even though it seems impossible, the fact is we're seated right next to him, right now. **How can that be?** Well, it's important to see things that pertain to our lives not only from a 3-dimensional view but also from a <u>spiritual view</u> as well…through the lens of God. Just as God sees us as washed clean and without sin, even though we're crummy sinners, so he sees us seated with his Son. <u>It's a spiritual reality</u>.

Listen, you know what it's going to take to live a life with God in it? It's going to take seeing life with <u>spiritual eyes</u>, just like we have to do with that verse and all the other promises in this book. If you're going to live a spiritual life, then you have to do spiritual things. Use your spiritual eyes.
If God says we're seated with his Son in the spiritual realm of his throne-room in heaven, then we need to believe it from a spiritual perspective. We need to see it through God's lens, not ours, and accept it by faith. That's what living by faith is about.

<u>**You might be thinking**</u> → *"Well, I don't know if I can. That's just pretty weird!"* → Yes, you can. I mean think about it; when an astronomer says there's a galaxy invisible to the human eye 8 billion light-years away, do you accept it as true? Yes. How do you accept it? By faith. After all…he's an astronomer, right? Just do the same with what God says. After all, he's the one who created that galaxy. So, we can trust him when he says we're seated with his Son in heaven right now, even though we're on earth. <u>One is a physical truth and the other is spiritual truth</u>.

And here's another thing: When you go to God for help and the help doesn't seem to come very quickly…if at all, don't say, *"Well, I guess we just never really know what God's going to do."* Yes, we do. God is not obscure with his Word. The answer may not be what we expect, but God will do what he says. Look at what he guarantees:

◈ **Isaiah 45:19** → *I, God, do not hide my words. No, I make bold promises of what I'm going to do, not hard-to-understand proclamations. I only speak what is true and reliable.*

God doesn't mince his words. He means what he says. So, take him at his word. When he says he'll help you...he'll do it.

◈ Remember **1 Kings 8:56**? → *Not one word has ever failed in all the promises God has given.*

Listen, agreeing with God's Word isn't easy. It's a matter of *choosing* to believe what he says and *acting* on it over and over again, in every circumstance, even if it seems crazy. Again, that's what faith is all about. And by doing that, guess what happens? It gets easier. That's what God means when he says in **2 Corinthians 5:7** *"We walk through each day by faith, not by how things may appear to us."*

Do you remember the story of the apostle Peter walking on water? He was doing fine until he started sinking. What caused him to sink? He saw the wind whipping up the waves and he became afraid. He went from bold faith (acting on Christ's invitation to join him walking on the water) to being afraid...and then sinking. But it wasn't the raging wind or the violent waves that defeated him...it was his <u>fear</u> of the wind and the waves. It was the sheer oddity and impossibility of walking on water that hit him. He took his eyes off Jesus. He looked at his circumstances and gave in to fear. <u>The result</u>? → Defeat. Mark my words, doubt and fear are definite *blessing-blockers*.

Don't let that happen to you. Don't take your eyes off the Promise-Giver only to focus on your circumstances. It may *seem* impossible that what he guarantees will actually come true, but that's where walking by faith, <u>not by how things *appear*</u> becomes real to us. So, live it out in your life. Walk by faith.

And always remember: God's the one who has *all* the right answers to *all* our problems. We don't have to guess at life. We just need to make him the source of our answers.

You might be wondering → *"Well, what if I don't have enough faith to believe what God promises?"*

That's ok. God knows you inside and out. He's not frowning at your unbelief. He's rooting for you. Don't forget, he's on your side. He wants you to win at life. **He just wants you to know** that to receive the guarantees of his promises, you'll have to use your faith.

Here's a big point: God's promises originate in the supernatural realm, so to receive them, we have to use a supernatural method → 'faith'. Our faith is what releases God's Word to work in our lives. You can see examples of that all through the Bible.

Just remember this: If we tell God our faith is weak and ask him to help our unbelief, that's exactly what he'll do. It won't be a magic pill. No, he'll put circumstances in our lives to grow our faith. We just need to *cooperate* with him when it happens and not avoid the hard stuff if that's part of the faith-growing process. Come on. We've got this. Let's get strong in our faith.

Here's a good way to build up faith in your heart: → Find a promise of God that speaks to your heart and fills your need. Then, meditate on it (think about it) and speak it out over and over again throughout the day and week, so you're hearing it. Do this until it starts to take root in your heart. Pretty soon you'll be speaking it with faith from the abundance of your heart.

Then when those arrows of the enemy start flying, you hold that shield of faith up and speak out God's Word, just like Jesus did to the enemy, when he was tested in the wilderness.

When trouble comes your way, and it will, here are two promises worth pondering and speaking out about:

2 Chronicles 32:8→ *We have God to help us win and to fight our battles for us.*
And

2 Chronicles 20: 17→ *You won't have to fight the battle. Just take up your position and stand there and watch God fight for you. He will deliver you.*

"*Bam!*" That's what I'm talking about. Think about it: God does the fighting for us...and we do the winning! Even though this verse was pertaining to a specific event back in the Old Testament, it's a general promise God makes to us all through the Bible. So, it applies to us as well...*if*...we receive it by faith.

Do you know when the real test of faith happens? It's trusting God's promises to come through even *before* the answers actually come. If God's promises take a lot longer to show up than you expected...keep your faith strong by reminding God daily of what he said he would do. He likes to hear it. He won't fail you. His timing is *always* perfect. Cross the finish line with faith, not doubt! Faith always passes the test of disappointment and the urge to give up. Doubt never does.

So, put this in your backpack as you walk-the-walk of God:

We have a standing invitation from God to approach his throne anytime we need to. And remember...God wants us to be confident and <u>bold</u> about it, just like he said four verses back. Go ahead, ask boldly and confidently expect him to come through. He loves to answer our prayers...especially when faith is backing them up.

What should we do with *trouble* when it comes?
Two Things

First...*Call* on God. Pay a visit to his throne room. He's already invited you.

Psalm 50:15 → *Call on me when you're going through distress or trouble. Do this and I will <u>rescue</u> you and you will end up <u>giving me glory</u>.*

The Hebrew word for '*<u>rescue</u>*' in this verse means '*to remove*'. This could mean God removing the trouble from us, or God removing us out of the trouble. Either way, we're rescued.

What should we do with that promise? → 3 things:
1. <u>Call out</u> to God. (Hebrew meaning – call out with urgency).
2. <u>Expect</u> him to rescue us because he says he will.
3. <u>Give</u> him the glory. (Don't forget to do this)

Warning - Let go and Let God. → So, often we miss out on what God wants to do for us _in_ our troubles because we get upset when he doesn't handle the problem the way we think he should. And when he doesn't rescue us according to our timing, we let our faith waver. We might sulk, or give up, or get angry at God, or we might just try to do things on our own to fix the situation rather than letting God accomplish what he wants while we're _in the middle_ of the ordeal.

As a result, we mess up what God was trying to do in our lives in the first place...making lemonade out of lemons. So, if God is squeezing you, stop messing with the blessing! No wavering or fixing it. Cooperate with him and get some lemonade out of it.

You might be thinking → _"Wait! What are you talking about? Where's the blessing in my troubles?"_

Well, God might have plans for you to grow and mature through your struggles. That's a blessing. Have you thought about that? I smile when I think back on how I would expect God to come through the way I wanted him to. But he decided to keep me in the trial longer than I wanted so he could teach me some stuff. Instead of accepting that, **I got upset with God.** I sulked. I took a break from him. It was a definite _blessing-blocker_ in my life, and truth be told, I missed out on a lot of opportunities for growth and blessings because of my immaturity. Don't let that happen to you. Stop messing with the blessing.

Secondly...Find your _refuge_ in Him

Not in distractions like TV, YouTube, Instagram, Facebook, Golf, etc. (Whoops. Did I say golf? Sorry, I'm not a golfer, so it's easy for me to say that. Ok...take golf off the list.)

Psalm 46:1 → _God is our refuge_ (in his presence is safety and rest and peace) _and he is our strength_ (meaning- his strength becomes our strength - physically, emotionally, and spiritually). _He is always ready to help us whenever we have trouble._

When trouble steps into our life, seek these 3 things:
1) Refuge from the storm
2) Strength to make it through
3) Help from a stronger source than us to fix it.

Luckily for us, God has volunteered for the job.

So, what do we do with that particular promise? → _3 things:_
1) Make God our _'refuge'_.
Easy enough. Right? But if I were to ask you how to do that, what would you say? I know...it's hard to verbalize, isn't it?
One answer would be, to get in his presence, because if you're right in the middle of his presence, you're safe and you can just rest, even while you're going through bad times. But, again, how do you do that? → **Get under his wings.**

Ⓧ **Psalm 57:1** → _Underneath your wings is where I will take refuge_ (meaning - like a chick under a mother hen's wings). _There I will feel safe until the trouble passes._

There are many verses throughout the Bible that say the same thing. Even Jesus quoted a Psalm while sitting overlooking Jerusalem. He said, _"Jerusalem, Jerusalem, how often I yearned to gather you under my wings, as a hen gathers her chicks, but you would not let me."_ (See Matthew 23:37)

Let's not be one of the _'would-nots'_. Let's get under his wings. That's the safest place to be when trouble comes our way. And, just like the first of those two verses says, let's stay there _until_ the trouble passes.

So, remember this: The safest place on earth during any trouble is being tucked right under God's wings.

Ⓧ **Psalm 73:28**: _It feels good for me to draw closer and closer to God, to come into his presence. I have made his presence my refuge_ (Hebrew meaning -- my dwelling place).

The end of that verse is important.→ Notice the words, _"I have made his presence my refuge."_ We must make the choice to do that for ourselves. Drawing closer to God is one thing, but _making_ his presence a place we _'dwell'_ in during the storm we're going through is a choice we alone have to make.
So **MAC** it. → **M**ake **A C**hoice to do that. Make his presence your refuge. Get under his wings.

You might be feeling → *"When I try to get into his presence, it just doesn't work. I don't feel at rest or at peace. All I feel is the worry and stress over the trouble I'm going through."*

Listen, I know exactly what that feels like. But we need make the *choice* to keep trying. Albert Einstein once said*, "You never fail until you stop trying."* Afterall, when you don't make a choice to keep trying, that itself is a choice, isn't it? Just ask God to help. He will. That's the kind of prayer he answers.

2) Make God's strength – our strength.

How do we do that? → First, we let go of trying to rely on our own strength, and then we ask for his supernatural strength. (It takes believing that God will give it.). **Then what?** We wait for it and expect it. In other words...we watch and wait. No impatience allowed. If God's giving it to us, then we don't have to struggle to get it. He's the one giving us strength.

Colossians 1:11 says → *God will make you stronger with his strength* (so that his strength is in you, and his strength becomes your strength). *Then, when trouble shows up, you'll have all the patience and endurance you'll need to make it through.*

Did you see it? It's not us but it's God who's making us stronger If you're like me, when you're going through troubles, you'll need all the strength, patience, and endurance you can get. Here's the thing → It'll either come from you or God. Which do you think would be the better source?

SIDENOTE: If someone were to ask you what the difference is between the word **patience** and the word **endurance**, would you know it?

Patience → means to tolerate someone or something without getting upset.
Endurance → means to tolerate adversity and trouble without giving up.

3) 'Let' God help.

Seems like a no-brainer, doesn't it? But you'd be surprised how many people struggle with the '*letting*' part. Either they don't know how to let go of control and let God take over, or they don't know how to open the door to God's help.

It may seem in your own life like the door to God's help is locked and you can't find the key. The good news is that God has a whole ring of keys that will unlock the doors to His help, His strength, His comfort, His wisdom...you name it. Those keys are found in His promises.

I'll tell you the <u>master key</u> that opens everything in the kingdom of God → _Believing_.
It's mentioned everywhere in God's Word, and to God, it's very important that we do it. But it's the _lack of belief_ that keeps many of us from receiving God's help. We struggle to _believe_ that he really will come through for us. I fully understand that feeling. I've been there myself many times. But nothing's going to change until we pick up that master key and use it.

<u>What is believing anyway?</u> Here's a verse with the answer:

✦ **Hebrews 11:1** → _Faith (Believing) is being <u>certain in our heart</u> that the things we hope will happen will actually come true. It's being convinced of their reality, even if we don't see them at the moment._

You probably already know this→ Faith is in us because God has given every believer a _"portion of faith"_ (See Romans 12:3). We just have to exercise it to make it grow. If our prayers are just words, without faith mixed in, well they may not rise any higher than our mouths. But when we put our faith behind our words, our prayers rise up to God, because God always honors faith.

Some people feel their prayers don't seem to reach heaven. But you wanna know something? Our prayers are just a breath away from God. Remember when Jesus said if we love him and obey him, then he and the heavenly Father will come and make their home in us (See John 14:23). God's in us. So, our prayers are not far from God at all. They're just a breath away. Check it out:

✦ **2 Corinthians 6:16** (God speaking) → _"I will live <u>in</u> them and I will walk <u>with</u> them and I will be their God and they will be my people."_

And this promise:

✦ **Romans 8:10→** _Christ the king lives <u>within you</u>, so you are made spiritually alive because God has fully accepted you and adopted you as his child...._

So, what does that tell us?→ The author of our faith lives within us and our prayers are just a breath away. He's just waiting to hear our words of faith. *Do you think faith is important? You better believe it.* (That's kind of a joke...but it's also true) ☺

Watch Out! Too many of us don't speak our faith. Instead, we speak our doubt.→ *"I don't feel very well." "I'm not very good at that." "I'm lonely." "No one cares about me."* You know what I say? Those are *'blessing-blockers'*. Why not speak what God is speaking, instead. I mean, his words are the real truth, right? So, let's say what he says. Let's let our words agree with God's. His words are spiritually alive, giving life to the hearer.

Look at what Jesus said about his words in John 6:63→ *"The words that I speak to you are spirit* (God-breathed) *and they are life* (they are living, alive in this world).*"*

Here's my point. Don't miss this. → When we speak out the promises of God, those words are in agreement with God. They are God-breathed words...meaning, they are alive and real in this earthly realm *because* God made them alive and real in the heavenly realm where they originated.

Think about this for a moment → When God spoke in the heavenly realm and said, *"Let there be light."* What happened? The light became real in the earthly realm. God spoke it and out of nothing, light appeared. When you speak out God's words, you're speaking words that originated in heaven and were intended to be a reality on earth. The thing that will make his words a reality in our own lives is – our faith.

Do you remember that verse on faith in Hebrews 11:1 four verses back? It said that *faith* is believing in the reality of that which we don't see. Just because we don't see it, doesn't mean it's not real. It is. Science has proven that.

Don't miss this either. → When we speak the promises of God, with faith mixed in, we're believing that the reality of those promises which originated in the spiritual realm will become reality for us in this earthly realm, even if we don't see it yet. Why? Because God already spoke them in the heavenly realm. The truth of his words already exist. They become real for us in this earthly realm through our faith. **That's what believing is all about, isn't it?**

So, never forget this → God wants our words to *agree* with his words. Speaking words of doubt *disagrees* with God's words. Don't let that happen. Make your words agree with what God says....not just for a few hours or a few days, but all the time. Afterall, didn't Jesus tell us to live by every one of God's words? We can't do that if we don't *agree* with what God's saying.

✦ **Matthew 4:4** Jesus talking→ *People don't live just by eating food alone, but they live their lives by every word that God says.*

You might be thinking → *"Yeah, well, I tried declaring the promises that God made, and my problems are still here. It didn't work for me."*

Wait a second. The trouble you're experiencing didn't change the Word of God. It's still the same. So, don't give up on his promises. Don't let your circumstances change your faith, let your faith change your circumstances.

✦ Here's that verse again: **2 Corinthians 5:7** → *The way we live this life* (as followers of God) *is by faith* (by believing God and what he says)*, not by how things may appear to us*.

Do you remember Jesus saying to the leper, *"Your faith has made you well again."* (See Luke 17:11), and to the blind man, *"According to your faith, receive your sight again."* (See Matthew 9:29).
It was their *faith* that <u>caused</u> God to respond to their need.
So, speak out God's promises with *faith* in your words. What will bring those promises to life in your life is your *faith* in what God said he would do.
God guarantees that his promises always get results. Remember this promise?

✦ **Isaiah 55:11** God speaking → *The words I speak and the promises I give will not return to me empty or without results. They will always accomplish what I intended them to do.*

God's promises will always go to work for you when you back them up with faith. But you know what people do? They wait and wait for God to work, and when he takes too long, they get discouraged and start to speak words of defeat. They let their circumstances bury their faith under a pile of doubt, impatience, and spiritual sulking. No wonder God's promises are rendered useless.

Be careful. Don't do that. There are many believers who never really experience God rescuing them out of trouble. Why is that? It's often because they get tired of waiting for God to act, so they take God's job away from him and start fixing it on their own, only to mess it up more.

Or, instead of walking close beside him day after day, they *wait* until trouble comes before they *finally* call on him for help.

And, because they haven't developed their faith, which comes from walking closely with God in the good times and the bad times, they don't quite know how to use faith when they really need it. Don't let that happen to you.

So, what do we do about it?

✦ James 4:8 → *Draw closer to God and He will draw closer to you*.

Here's the thing → If we want God to rescue us in the bad times, then we have to get close to him in the good times. Why? Because God responds to our faith...not just our needs.

We have to develop our faith so we're ready to use it when we really need it. It's *our* belief and trust in his wisdom, his abilities, and his power that moves him to respond, not just because we're in a bad situation.

Just remember: We'll never be able to develop the trust and faith we need in tough times if we don't spend the time drawing close to him in the good times.

And don't forget, seeking help from God isn't a Hail-Mary pass at the last minute just because we're in a bind. According to that verse, it's all about getting to know God by drawing closer to him.

Think about that for a moment. The more we get to know God, the more we'll trust him, and that opens the floodgates for him to help us. If God is a stranger to us, just some entity we pray to only when we need help, then our faith will be weak. Doubt may creep in, and it will hinder God's help from flowing to us. He needs to be up-close and real to us and that will only happen if we seek him diligently, carefully, and consistently.

Is prayer your steering wheel or your spare tire? Corrie Ten Boom

Here's another thing I need to bring up:
Trouble often comes our way because of <u>attacks from the spiritual realm</u>. How often have you found yourself drawing closer to God and *"bam!"*, coming out of left-field, you get smacked in the head with trouble you didn't ask for? Why is that? It's because you're one of God's children and that makes you an enemy of those fallen angels God talks about, who hate him. Why do they hate God? Because God cast them out of heaven after of their rebellion against him, dooming them to an eternity of darkness and separation from all things good. So, they lash out at God's children since they can't touch God directly.

Never forget that we're fighting spiritual battles as well as the battles of this life in the earthly realm. And the invisible entities we're fighting against are described by the apostle Paul (in Ephesians 6:12) as evil rulers of the unseen realm, strong powers of darkness, and spiritual forces of wickedness. These enemies of our soul are no lightweights. They mean business. They are out to destroy God's kids – that's us. So, don't ignore them. They are out for revenge. That's why Paul tells us to put on and <u>wear God's spiritual armor</u>, so we can withstand the attacks of these spiritual forces. That's what armor does. It helps prevent the enemy from harming us.

Can you picture yourself walking around with a helmet and a breastplate and a sword? Me neither, but don't worry, it's invisible. It's God's *spiritual* armor, and that's what we're supposed to wear if we don't want to be spiritually defeated.

Make sure you use the '<u>shield of faith</u>' that Paul mentions as part of that armor (See Ephesians 6:16). It's meant to shield you from the arrows of your enemy. But how often do we forget about our shield and leave it in the closet? We then get pierced with one of those arrows, and now we're wounded and out of the fight. We can't be victorious in our troubles when that happens.

In the middle of our trouble, how does the shield of faith actually work? This next verse has the answer:

Ephesians 6:16→ *Pick up the shield of faith. Hold it up so you can stop the flaming arrows of the evil-one.*

The shield of faith only works when you pick it up and hold it up. It won't do you any good if it's lying on the ground. What are you holding it up for? To protect yourself from the flaming arrows the enemy is firing at you. Notice these arrows are flaming. Why aren't they just plain arrows? Because plain arrows can cause wounds, but flaming arrows set your life on fire, making the damage (trouble) done to you far worse.

Remember what Jesus told us? → **The enemy has these three goals in mind:**
1) to steal from us (things like happiness, peace, security, etc.)
2) to destroy and ruin our life.
3) to kill us (through danger and illness etc.).

You know what else we need to watch out for? → Our own words. Look at what Jesus said:

Matthew 12:34 → *What we say with our mouths comes from what's filling our hearts.*

Let me ask you this → What's filling your heart? What are you telling yourself or others about your troubles? Does it build your faith up, or is it tearing it down?

When it comes to overcoming our troubles, our words won't work without faith any more than our faith won't work without our words. If our heart is full of faith, we'll speak like it. And just the opposite can be true. If our heart is full of doubt, we'll speak it. Many of us don't realize that, so we continue to speak words of doubt and unbelief without realizing how it's affecting our faith. We tell our friends and family how big our problems are instead of how big our God is. All that does is weaken our faith. That's a *'blessing-blocker'*. Don't let that happen to you.

So, remember this → It's not the words we speak that make the difference, it's what's filling our hearts. Is there faith or doubt _behind our words_? The results depend on it...whether to our benefit, or our detriment.

You might be asking → *"Well, what if I feel I don't have enough faith to actually speak words of faith?"*

I get it, and I'm with you on that, but does that mean we shouldn't start speaking with faith until we have enough faith to back it up? Nope. Speaking out God's Word helps our faith grow. Remember that man in Mark 9:24, who asked Jesus to heal his child? He said, *"Lord, I believe. But help me with my unbelief."* He wasn't sure he had enough faith either, yet Jesus answered the man's request and healed the child. Jesus didn't wait until the man had enough faith. He accepted the man's faith where it was at, and God will meet your faith where it's at as well.

 Not only that, but it's God's Word that does the work, not the one quoting it. The power is in his Word, not us. Our faith simply activates his Word. Remember I mentioned that Jesus often said things like, *"Your faith has made you whole"* or *"Your faith has healed you"* or *"Let it be according to your faith"*. How can that be? Wasn't it God doing the healing? Yes, but it was the person's faith that was the catalyst to activate it.

Here's a good way to build up faith in your heart: Find a promise of God that speaks to your heart and fills your need. Then, meditate on it and speak it out until it starts to take root and fills your heart. Pretty soon you'll be speaking it from the abundance of your heart.

Then when those flaming arrows of the enemy start flying, hold that shield of faith up and speak God's Word with as much faith as you have in your heart. God sees your heart and he'll honor your faith right where you're at. The enemy will flee.

Here's a powerful weapon Jesus used against the enemy:

He used what God calls the <u>Sword of the Spirit</u> which, according to the Bible, is the Word of God (See Ephesians 6:17). It's the offensive weapon that you stab and slice the enemy with. When Jesus was attacked by the enemy, he replied, *"It is written."* Then he would quote God's Word. The enemy couldn't take the truth because he's a liar, and according to Jesus, there's not an ounce of truth in him. But he didn't flee immediately. He kept badgering Christ. Jesus didn't give up, though. He knew the power of God's Word. He just kept slicing and jabbing with that Sword – *"It is written..."* and then he would quote God's words again. Over and over he did this until the enemy gave up and fled. That's what will happen to us. So, pick up the *Sword of the Spirit* and use it. Slice and stab the enemy with it until he flees from you.

Here's a key point → Even though Jesus quoted scripture to fight the enemy, it wasn't God's Word alone that made the sword so effective, it was his faith in God's Word. Don't forget that. Put your faith into God's Word and speak it out against the enemy. As one of our granddaughters says..."*rememberize it*".

Ever seen a dad get so upset when his son or daughter is getting picked on by a bully? He wants to step in and fight the battle for his child. That's what God wants to do for us when the enemy picks on us. And, when God enters the fight, he never loses...ever! Here's a guarantee for you:

<u>2 Chronicles 32:8</u>→ *We have God to fight our battles for us and to help us <u>win</u>.*

It doesn't say we have God to help us so we *'might'* win. No God's there *"to help us win"*. Remember, he's doing the fighting for us, so what's the outcome? <u>We win</u>! Why is that? Because God always wins. Now, speak that stuff out. → *"God you say, you're in the battle along with me, fighting the battle for me. And, because you always win, <u>I know</u> I'll win..."* → **That's faith!**

I like this next promise:

✦ **2 Chronicles 20: 17**→ *You won't have to fight the battle. Just* take up your position *and* stand there *and* watch *God fight for you and deliver you.*

That's what God guarantees us! We do our part, which is what? → Getting in a battle stance, ready to fight if we need to, and then what? → We *watch* God fight for us.
Notice we're *both* involved. God and us. God loves to help us, but he wants to know that we're *in-it-to-win-it* as well.

🌲**I want you to Get this. It's important** → We need to follow the example of Abraham in the Old Testament. God made a bunch of promises to him that seemed impossible to actually come true. But this is what Abraham did with those promises:

✦ **Romans 4:17** → *Abraham* believed *that God could bring the dead back to life, and that* God could call into existence those things that aren't even a reality yet.

Wow!!! Think about that for a moment. That's faith in action! That's what we need to do when we're in the middle of trouble – believe that God can call into existence that which is not real yet. That's amazing! Don't move on until you've digested that truth. That's the level of faith God wants us to live in.

🌲**There's something else I need to mention here:**
There is trouble that also comes our way because of the wrong choices we make in our lives.

Maybe you've heard the phrase: *"We are where we are in our lives today because of the choices we've made in the past."* **This is where it gets tricky.** → Did God bring on the trouble we're encountering?...or did evil spiritual forces?...or was it us?

Many people say → *"Why did God let this happen to me?"* Here's what we have to get a grasp on.→ People often just assume that when bad things happen to them that God must have caused it. After all, if he's in control and his will is always done, then he must have caused it. Right?

The thing is, God doesn't always get to have his way in our lives. Why? Because <u>we often won't let him</u>. He won't force us to go his way. He'll do everything he can to reach out to us, but if we're not listening, or if we ignore his nudges, then he'll just let us go our own way, even if it's going to lead us right smack dab into trouble.

God isn't going to *force* his people to take part in his plan to bless and protect them. So, if we move out of his sphere of blessings and protection, then we're going to be more vulnerable to trouble coming our way.

And what's funny is that when the trouble comes, people then complain, *"Why did God let this happen to me?"* → God didn't do it to them... most likely they did it to themselves.

Listen, God always *keeps* his promise to bless and protect us.
But you know what keeps God's blessings away? → Yup. If he tells us to go one way (to keep us out of trouble) and we continue to go the opposite, things aren't going to go so well for us.

✦ <u>Hebrews 3:12</u> → *Watch out and be careful that unbelief and sin-bent desires don't lead you off the path of following God*.

In other words: <u>Stop messin' with the blessin' of protection</u>!

Some people think → *"Well, if God's so good and he cares about us so much, then why doesn't he just go ahead and bless us and protect us anyway?"*

I'm sure the answer won't shock you. God's goodness prevents him from blessing or protecting something that's wrong, even if he loves us when we're doing what's wrong.

But I want you to get this: No matter how much trouble we've gotten ourselves into, or how far down the wrong path we've gone, <u>here's the answer</u>: Ready for it? → **God allows U-turns**. It's as simple as that. If you've found you've been running away from him, just turn around and start running toward him...all the way until you run into his welcoming arms.

If you've stepped outside of God's plan of blessings, and you're sorry you did, then make a U-turn and step right back into it again. Tell God what you did and ask his forgiveness. That's what God calls *'repentance'*. He's always ready to welcome you back and start blessing you again. The Bible makes that clear over and over again, just so we don't miss it.

We have to get away from the notion that God's continually disappointed or unhappy with us when we mess up. We can fall into the trap of thinking if anything bad happens to us, it must be God spanking us for being bad. But that's not the heart of God. After all, he made us. He understands us. He knows our weaknesses inside and out. And he sent the Holy Spirit to live within us so he could help us, encourage us, and strengthen us. That's how much he cares about helping us. But many believers don't have confidence in this because they've never fully grasped the depth of God's love and absolute goodness towards them.

Here's a guarantee we've already covered, but it also rings true here, especially if the trouble we're in is our own doing:

Psalm 37:5 → *Commit everything you do to the Lord.* (Hebrew meaning-- roll each one of your concerns off of you and onto God). *Trust him with it all. Do that and **he will help you*** (Hebrew meaning – He will work it all out for you. He will attend to it and put it all in order).

The cool thing about God is that he's able to turn any situation around and work it all out for our good. Any situation! And he loves to do it. All he's waiting for is for us to give him the chance. So, don't be messing with the blessing. Get on the right path that leads you right back into his plan of blessings for your life and let him turn the lemons into lemonade.

You might be wondering → *"Well, what if I didn't cause the trouble? What if it was because of..."*

Then we need to trust that God knows what's going on and that he'll work it all out for our good. Do you remember this verse?

Romans 8:28 → *We know* (Greek meaning- we are convinced of this with absolute certainty) *that if we truly love God, he will cause* *each and every detail of our lives to work* together (blended and woven together) *so that it turns out for our good*.

Are you convinced of this promise with absolute certainty? If so, then sit back, rest, and let God work it all out. **If you're not the cause**, then there's no U-turns needed. Just 'Let go and Let God'. He says he'll work it all out to your benefit, so let him. Or, are you going to get in the way and try to fix it yourself?

Keep in mind: It may take a little time for God to lead you out of the trouble and turn it all around, but you can be absolutely certain that he'll do it according to his plan and his timing, not yours. It may or may not be the way you wanted it to work out, but it will *always* be for your good. He promises it. Besides, he's madly in love with you and wants nothing but good for you...all of the time. So, whatever the end-result is, you can be certain it will be good.

Are you _confident_ in God when trouble comes?

This next verse is something we can speak out ourselves:

Psalm 16:8 → *Because I continually set the Lord before me, I know <u>with certainty</u> that he is close by my side. And <u>because I know</u> he's right beside me, <u>I will not be shaken</u> or defeated when* **trouble** *comes*.

That's one confident statement! Would you like that kind of confidence when trouble comes your way? I know I would.

Here's the thing, though.→ None of us would probably admit it, but sometimes we act like God's not there...at all. In the midst of our troubles, we might say with our mouths, *"I know God's with me."* but we sometimes don't say it with our actions. It's almost the opposite. We get frustrated with God, so we give up and do what *we* want. We disobey a little here, a little there. It's as if our actions are saying, *"God's not really there beside me"*. Wanna know how I know this? I speak from experience.

But why was the writer of this verse so <u>confident</u> that God was right beside him during his troubles? It's because he <u>continually</u> put God in front of him, in the forefront of his thoughts and actions. He was feeding his faith and starving his doubt. So, even in the middle of trouble, he was unbendable, unshakable, and full of confidence.

In your personal life, how do you continually *'set God before you'*? If you're not sure, don't worry, here's a way:

Isaiah 26:3 → *God will* keep in complete and total peace all *those who...let their thoughts be fixed on him* (instead of their worries, troubles, or fears).

This is a method for keeping God in front of us. We fix our thoughts on him, here and there, throughout the day, feeding our faith, not our doubts. We keep our focus on him, not our troubles. This will give us more and more confidence to trust him in the middle of the storm; and in return, God will keep us in total peace throughout the ordeal. Try it. See for yourself.

And think about this. For God to keep *you* in a state of peace, he has to zero-in on *you* personally, taking an interest in what's going on in *your* life, taking the time to help you stay in a state of peace amidst your troubles. We're talking about the creator of the universe getting personally involved here. After all, he's got the universe to keep going. Right? Why would he bother with measly little *you*? It's because he's madly in love with you. You're his child. Nothing's going to keep his love away.

How about this statement of confidence:

Psalm 23:4 → Even *when I walk through dark valleys in my life* (feeling unsafe, unsure, not knowing what's ahead), *I will not be worried or afraid* (a faith choice), *for you are close beside me and your shepherd's staff protects and guides me.*

There it is again - a bold and confident statement by the writer of that verse, about not being shaken, knowing that God is right there beside him, guiding him and protecting him.

Not to be redundant here, but what are you going to do with this promise and the one before it? Are you going to just read them and move on? Or, are you going to claim those promises for yourself, speaking them out with confidence, just like those writers did – that God will keep you in total peace and that he'll be right beside you through your troubles? **MAC** it- Make A Choice.

SIDE-NOTE: **Do you know what a shepherd's staff was for?** Yup, to guide the sheep. But it was also to fight off the enemy when it attacked one of the sheep. *Whack!* That's what our shepherd will do for us...*if* we stay close to him. When you think about it, that's pretty cool. So, claim it.

Here's a final point worth mentioning:

Get used to the idea that you live on planet earth, and you're going to have troubles, even if it's not your fault. If you can accept that, then the next thing you need to decide on is what you're going to do while you're in the *middle* of the trouble. This next verse has the answer:

James 1:2 → *When you run into a lot of problems, or encounter a bunch of trouble and trials, consider it a reason to be glad it's happening, because it's going to challenge your faith. And when you make it through the trouble, still holding onto your faith, you'll be even stronger when more trouble comes down the road.*

Those two words - "consider it" are the key. That's the choice we have to make – How are we going to *consider* the situation we're in? Are we going to look at our crummy circumstances as a chance to let God teach us and then grow from them...or...are we going to complain and be inwardly angry at God for letting that stuff happen to us? The choice is ours to make. Make A Choice how you'll consider your troubles. **MAC** it.

You might be asking → *"So, if it's not me causing the trouble, and it's not God causing the trouble, then what is it?"*
Look at what Jesus said:

John 16:33→ *I've told you these things, so you'll realize that in me you will have peace. In the world we live in, you will have troubles. But I want you to be encouraged, for I have overcome the world.*

The world we live in can just plain cause us trouble. Not God, not you...the *'world'*. Why? Because there's sin in it.

You might be wondering→ *"What did Jesus mean by the "world", and what does he mean that he overcame the world?"*

The *'world'* in the Bible, refers to the earth under the dominion of the evil-one (that fallen angel that Jesus called Satan). The *'world'* is comprised of sin, evil, and rebellion against God and it's operating outside of God's divine influence, authority and protection.

You might be wondering → *I don't get it, how exactly did Jesus overcome the 'world'?*

He did it by conquering sin, and evil, and death. How? By volunteering to die on that Roman cross for mankind's rebellion, the cause of those things entering this world in the first place. He took *our* place on death row, satisfying God's judgment against our wrongdoing. **And what was that judgment?** It was the pronouncement of eternal separation from God's presence and everything good that comes from him...forever.

But here's the cool thing, Jesus destroyed this eternal death sentence with his resurrection. By him coming back to life again, *death* completely lost its power over him. And since we're united with Jesus, death has lost its power over us as well. That's what God says. We'll leave death behind when we're resurrected and given eternal life along with a new body fit for eternity just like Jesus (See 2 Corinthians 5).

Yes, we'll physically die because of the effects of sin on our earthly bodies, but, according to God, our spirits get to live in a new body that he'll give us, just like the one he gave Jesus, but it will be our very own, fit to be with him forever in a kingdom that's going to be better than a thousand Disney Worlds (Ok, yeah...I know I said Disney World...not Disneyland. Sorry, I let my personal preference take over.☺)

You know what? If I weren't a believer, I would think what I just wrote is utter nonsense...and pretty weird at that. But listen, I didn't dream this stuff up...God did. I'm just sharing what he said in his Word. It's his plan, not mine. So, why would we doubt it? I mean, why is it that we can believe in quantum physics, black holes, and distant galaxies that we can't even see, and must take it on blind faith, but yet, we can't believe in the spiritual realities that God talks about?

You might also be thinking → *"Ok, if Jesus did all that, then how come there's still so much evil and death in the world?"*

You wanna know the answer? Here it is:
There are basically two kingdoms operating on this earth right now, and God has allowed it to be so. Soon, in the near future, when God sends the enemies of our souls to their eternal doom, there will be only one kingdom – God's kingdom. But right now, God is allowing his own kingdom to operate and he's allowing Satan's kingdom to function at the same time. There's a reason for that. God is using it for his purposes, whether to show us there's good and there's evil, to point us to himself, or for some other very good reason. He knows what he's doing and since that's the case, he is allowing evil to continue...for now.

You might be asking → *"Wait a second! Why would God even allow 'evil' to operate on this earth at all, especially since it's causing so much destruction and pain?"*

He didn't and he wouldn't. The first two people God created did. They gave up their right of authority over the earth that God had given them, and they gave that authority over to the evil-one when they gave in to his temptation.

I'll tell you what happened. When God created mankind, he gave them dominion over the earth. God's original design was for humans to govern his creation with moral goodness, in obedience to his instructions and his will. Consequently, humanity would live under God's care and abundant blessings.

God had warned them though, of the consequences of partaking in wrongdoing. But earth's first two human beings, Adam and Eve, had free-will and they chose to disregard God's instructions and instead gave in to the deception of the evil-one. The consequence of their choice (the judgment that followed, just as God warned) was spiritual death, death of their bodies, and separation from God and his blessings...forever.

You might also be questioning → *Why is this evil-one even around?*

The Bible says because of Satan's rebellion, God banished him from heaven and cast him and all the angels who followed him to earth, when the earth was still formless, long before God brought forth His creation. (See Revelation 12:9)

It's a little complicated, but let me try to make it simple:
Sometime before God created mankind, He created spiritual creatures (angels) of different levels of power, forms, and function, to operate in the heavenly realm. God doesn't need any help governing the universe, but he likes to share his power and authority. These angels served God's purposes in the administration of his creation. Some of these angels were pretty weird looking too, with multiple eyes and wings and other stuff.
One of these angels was high up in the hierarchy of angels. His name was Lucifer. (See Ezekiel 28: 14,16) but later his name was changed to Satan (which means *'adversary'*) (See Job 1:6-9 and Matthew 4:10).

Before he rebelled against God, Lucifer was an angelic creature, created by God to be very wise and quite stunning to look at, a spectacle of flawlessness, and was honored above all angels, with great authority and wisdom; a leader of God's angels (See Ezekiel 28: 14,16). The Bible says of Lucifer, *"You were blameless in all of your ways <u>until</u> the point that <u>evil</u> was found in you."*

Because of his lofty position of authority and wisdom among the angels, arrogance filled Lucifer to the point he thought he could rule the angels *"like God, the most high"* (See Isaiah 14:14). He forgot that he was a created one, not the Creator himself. In the process of his rebellion against God, around a third of the angelic creatures decided to follow him. As a consequence, God cast Lucifer from heaven and threw him and the fallen angels that followed him, (now called *'demons'*) to the formless earth (not like the earth we know today). There they dwelt in oblivion.

Sometime later, God then decided to give form to the formless earth, and create mankind along with all of creation, and to humanity he gave dominion over the earth (See Genesis 1:26,28).

Satan was enraged with God for taking his domain on earth away from him, and since he knew the judgment of eternal doom had been placed on him by God, he thought stealing mankind's new dominion over the earth would be like spitting in God's eye.

So, he stole back control of the earth by deceiving the first man and woman who bought into his lie and followed his temptation. As a result of their disobedience to God, the first two people on earth lost their authority over the earth that God had given them, as well as the *full* blessings of God that went with it.

When Satan tempted Christ in the wilderness, he reminded Jesus that Adam had relinquished his authority over the earth. He said to Jesus, *"I will give you all these kingdoms of this earth and all the power and authority that comes with it, for it has been relinquished (given over) to me."*

Jesus said this earth is Satan's kingdom, for now (See John 14:30). He called it *"the world"*. And, according to Jesus, all who refuse to follow God are under the dominion of '*this world*' controlled by Satan. He said if they refuse to let God restore them to their original sin-free state of innocence, through God's forgiveness of sin, they will follow the same demise as the evil-one and all the fallen angels – eternal separation from God and from all things good.

The beautiful thing is, God has lovingly done everything he could to keep people from following in Satan's demise, by offering them a pardon for their sin and giving them eternal life, but many choose not to accept God's conditions for living with him forever. They would rather go their own way, not God's.

When Jesus said he had '*overcome the world*', it was a declaration that this was just the beginning of Satan's defeat, that God was restoring mankind and earth to His original plan.

Satan thought he had mankind forever under his power. When God sent Jesus (whom the Bible calls "the second Adam") to die for our sins, it was a complete surprise to Satan. Never could he imagine that God would go to such an extent to suffer at his own hand just to get mankind back. That's because he could not comprehend the amazing love of God has for us.

Why do I bring all of this up?

Here's why → Too many people I encounter, who follow God, know very little as to the origin of the enemy. They usually know the enemy's out to get them, but that's about the extent of it. They just think there's some cosmic war going on between good and evil, between God and the devil. And many don't even believe there's an evil-one to begin with, nor a Hell of eternal separation from God's presence and all things good.

Here's the way I see it → If Jesus said many times that Satan and Hell are real, and that he, Jesus, came to destroy the works of the evil-one, and save us from Hell, then we have to decide if Jesus was lying to us when he mentioned these things...or...that he was telling us the truth.

Bottomline: It's this enemy of our soul who wants to reap destruction in our lives, make us miserable, and give us all kinds of trouble.

So.....*"Why did God let this happen to me?"* → It's not God.

Getting back to the topic of 'trouble'

If the trouble you're encountering has its source in the enemy, then I would recommend you make good use of the promises in this book. They are your weapons of choice. 1 Peter 5:9 tells us to fight back against the evil-one, being firm in our faith. That word *'resist'* in the Greek means to set ourselves against, to forcefully oppose the enemy. We have to have a weapon in our hand to do that, and according to Ephesians 6:17, God's Word is like a *sword* that can be used against the evil one. So, stab and lunge with those promises. Hit the enemy with the truth. He's a liar at heart and he can't defend against it.

But if we haven't been practicing our swordplay each day, we'll be much more vulnerable to wounds from the enemy. You don't want that. So, practice, practice, practice. Use the sword of God's Spirit...the truth.

God's promises are truth and light, and we are now children of light who have the truth inside us. Just like darkness can't defeat light, lies can't defeat truth. The enemy has absolutely no defense against truth, so he will flee. Think about that. Jesus said in John 8:44 that the evil-one has always hated truth and that there is no truth found in him. No *truth* at all found in him. Wow, that's crazy to think about. So, use God's promises like a sword. They're nothing but truth. The enemy will flee from it.

And consider this: James 4:7 reminds us to surrender our '*self*' to God, instead of letting '*self*' give in to the enemy. That's important. If our '*self*' isn't surrendered to God, then we're left in a vulnerable position. But, if we're surrendered to God, we can resist the enemy from a place of power. We're no longer succumbing to Satan's deceit. He'll have no choice but to flee.

That's how we deal with the enemy that's invisibly causing trouble in our lives.

You are the victor...not the victim.

TRUSTING GOD
What God Guarantees If You Do

Trusting someone we know is obviously easier than trusting someone we've never seen. Although God is invisible to us, he's very real, and there is no greater way to show our belief in him than by trusting him.

One of the best ways I know to learn to trust God is to become familiar with his promises. They reveal his heart to us, showing us how much he loves us and wants to help us.

So, what does God guarantee if we <u>trust</u> him?

Here is a wonderful <u>promise</u>:

Psalm 32:10 → *Those who truly <u>TRUST</u> God* (who fully rely on him, totally confident in his wisdom, his ways, his abilities, and his power...thus having no worries or fears), *to them **his love*** (his guiding, providing, protecting love), *and **his kindness*** (his goodwill and good intentions), ***and his goodness*** (his supernatural favor in the giving of good things that will help them thrive, not just survive, but thrive and prosper and do well in life); *these things will <u>surround</u> and <u>fill</u> their lives...all <u>because</u> they trust him.*

I would suggest really digesting this promise. Don't pass it by. There are huge blessings in it. If you truly <u>trust</u> him the way that verse says, God guarantees he'll do **3 things for you**:

1.) His '<u>*love*</u>' will surround and fill your life.

The word '*love*' in the Old Testament Hebrew language is "<u>chesed</u>" and it describes love the way a father would love his children. What does a kind, loving father do for his children? He lovingly <u>provides</u> for them, and gives them loving <u>guidance</u>, and he lovingly <u>protects</u> them.

So, if you're doing what this verse says, truly trusting God, then look for those things throughout the day. Expect God to provide for you, to guide you, and protect you just as a loving father would do. And then, watch what happens. Be patient and watch. God doesn't lie.

2.) His '_kindness_' will surround and fill your life.

This is above and beyond the usual kindness God shows everybody. This is aimed directly at you in such a concrete way that you won't be able to miss it, simply because you trust him.

This is also part of that Hebrew word "chesed". It includes 'goodwill and good intentions' and that's what God will have toward you – nothing but kindness and the best intentions..._if_ you're truly trusting him. If you're doing that...truly trusting him, then look for and expect God's good intentions throughout the day directly aimed at you. You'll be amazed at the stuff that happens. After all, it's a promise God made, and he never breaks his promises. So, expect it.

3.) His '_goodness_' will surround and fill your life. (the giving of good things)

Many Bible scholars include the word "_goodness_" when translating the Hebrew word "chesed". In that verse we just read, it means God is very good to those who truly trust him.
In the original Hebrew language, it means God will give them good things that will help them to thrive, not just survive, but thrive and prosper and do well in life.

So, if you're truly trusting God, then you too can expect good things to show up in your everyday living, to help you thrive and prosper and do well in life. Look for it to happen.

Just remember – All through his Word, God makes promises to us so that we'll benefit from them. They won't do us any good if we don't use them. So, don't let them pass you by.

Note: We in Western societies often think the words to prosper and to receive blessings and good things means to get rich and have a lot of material possessions. But, in the Old Testament culture, it has a broader meaning. → To make progress favorably in all areas of your life; to do well in life – relationally, materialistically, financially, and spiritually.

🎒 **Put this in your backpack on your journey through life: I don't want you to miss it...so let's review**:
* Do you want God's favor to <u>surround</u> and <u>fill</u> your life daily?
* Do you need his loving <u>guidance</u>?
* Do you need him to <u>provide for you</u>?
* Do you need him to <u>protect you</u> (in little or big things)?
* Do you want him to <u>help you prosper</u> and <u>do well in life</u>?

All you have to do is <u>trust</u> him.... really, truly trust him for every little and big thing in your life. That's it! And then watch and wait for it to surround you and fill your life. God won't let you down because you're faithfully trusting him. <u>Watching and waiting are a part of faith. Never forget that</u>.

Keep in mind – All through his Word, <u>trusting him</u> is a big deal...I mean, it's a HUGE deal to God. Don't take it lightly. We're so used to controlling our lives that it's hard to put anything that really concerns us into God's hands and then completely let go of it, trusting him with it. We tend to take it back again and try to make it all work out ourselves, especially if we think God is being too slow. Then we realize what we're doing, and we give it back to him once again...for a while, and then we grab it back once more, over and over again.

You know what? God understands. He just smiles at us and tries to remind us that he has perfect timing and that he can handle things on his own without our help. He just wants us to believe it, trust it, and rest in it.

> *A man says, "Show me and I'll trust you."*
> *God says, "Trust me and I'll show you."* (anonymous)

There's another thing we get hung up on:
We tend to want him to fix the problem <u>the way we want it fixed</u>. But God's way of doing things isn't always our way of doing things, and the sooner we accept that fact, the more we'll let go and let God do what he wants, while we get on with the business of watching for his blessings. So...*let go and let God.*

Here's a promise about 'trusting' God for guidance.

Proverbs3:5,6 → *Put all of your <u>trust</u> in God with everything that's in you. Don't just rely on your own understanding of the situations you're encountering. In all your ways* (your plans, your paths, the decisions you make) *acknowledge God* (invite him into the middle of all your situations). *Do this and <u>he will guide and direct your steps</u>, levelling and smoothing out the paths.*

I think many of us find it hard to trust anyone else's judgment but our own when it comes to certain situations in our lives. We forget to invite God into the middle of our circumstance. So, who ends up directing our steps? We do. We just keep pushing our way along, expecting God to bless us, even though he's been left behind in the dust. This is where many people miss out on God's blessings. It would be foolish to manipulate the circumstances just to get what we want. Either God's in control...or...we are. **Which is it for you?**

It's interesting when you look at the Hebrew meaning of the word *"<u>direct</u>"* at the end of that promise, when it says God will <u>direct</u> our paths. The word not only means to lead and guide, but it also means to level out and make smooth the rough terrain on the path you're taking. So, if the road God's directing you to travel on is rocky or rough, just know God will smooth it out and level it off for you. The going will get easier. He guarantees it.

How would you like to <u>not lack</u> anything that's good in your life? Trust is involved.

Psalm 34:10 → *Those who truly <u>seek</u> the* Lord (out of hunger to know him, and by getting to know him, they trust him); *<u>they will not lack any good thing</u>.* (Hebrew meaning→ their lives will be <u>filled with good things</u> – things that are pleasant and will help them thrive and prosper and do well in life).

Seeking God (to know him, to understand his ways), is another big thing to God, a really BIG thing to him. And he will honor us with good things if we do.

Seeking God will always lead to _trusting_ him more. Why? Because the more we get to know someone the more we'll trust them. It's the same way with God...we'll _trust_ him more.

Bottom-line: I want a life <u>filled</u> with good things, don't you? Not just surviving but thriving and doing well in life. God says that's what he wants to give us, and he will, if we seek to knw him and learn to trust him. What could stop that from happening? Yup...you got it..._not_ seeking him and _not_ trusting him.

Don't let the naysayers tell you that God doesn't work that way. Yes, he does. He wants your life filled with good things. Read the words in that promise again. What is there to misunderstand? Nothing. It's written all through the Bible. So, jump in. <u>Really seek to know God</u> and <u>truly trust him</u> (completely 'let go and let God'; get out of the way and let him work in your life). Do this and he'll take good care of you. → <u>You won't lack good things in your life</u>...because you seek him and trust him.

But here's the thing. → There's not one good thing that God couldn't give us _if_ he wanted to. However, he knows what's good for us and what's not good for us. And not only that, we have to remember what's good for someone else may not be what's good for us. So, instead of telling God what we think we need, why not just _let go_ and trust him to give us what he _knows_ we need.

'Letting go' is hard, isn't it? Why is that? Could it be that we don't really trust that God knows what's best for us like we do, especially when God takes us into troubled waters, not to drown us, but to teach us? Are we afraid to let that happen because he might throw something difficult into our lives to teach us how to trust him? Is that why we try to control our lives so much, why we won't _'let go and let God'_? Hmmm. ☺

Bottomline: It really does just boil down to that one simple word that's packed with so much meaning..._trust_...trusting him.

Just consider this: God is always good to us, not just some of the time... _all_ the time. He <u>always</u> wants the best for us, so he gives us what he _knows_ will help us and bless us. We may not like what he gives us, but he knows what's best.

So, what are you personally going to do? Are you going to '_let go_' and trust God to give you what he _knows_ you need? You know what I say? → Make a choice. **MAC** it.

Think about this for a moment → God never changes. Right? I mean, he's the same today as he was 4,000 years ago. So, way back in Exodus, in the days when the Israelites were leaving Egypt to go to the Promise Land (that place that the 10 spies reported on...the land that God described as rich with abundance and was theirs for the taking, free of charge), all they had to do was _trust_ that God knew what was best for them and just follow his instructions even when the going was rough. It's the same for us today. Just trust and obey and he'll lead the way. Again, <u>God makes his way of living simple...it's us who seem to make it hard</u>.

And don't forget, that through the wilderness, he provided food and water, and their clothes and shoes never wore out.... for 40 years!!! **Yeah, baby**...that's some durable camping gear! They don't make it like that anymore.☺ <u>They didn't lack anything</u>, not a single thing...in that desolate wasteland of a wilderness (see Deuteronomy 8:3,4). And that wasn't even the promised land where all the really good stuff was waiting for them. So, what are we worried about? He'll do the same for us when we're in the wildernesses of life.

You know what? You and I go through dry parched deserts in our own lives, full of rough terrain and struggles, and God is willing and able to take good care of us as we go through them. Right? So, what did he want from the Israelites back then, and what does he want from us today? → <u>Trust</u>....to trust that he knows what's best for us. That's it. Could it be any easier? No, Nien, Nu, Nej, Nai, Nee, Non, Nao...Nope.☺

Want some good things from God? Then look at this next guarantee:

Lamentations 3:25 → *God is good* (he gives good things) *to those who seek him* (those who seek him diligently, carefully, and consistently, out of hunger to know him). *Consequently, as a result of seeking him, they wait for God to act with expectation, confidence, and trust in him.*

You can see that God is pretty clear on what he requires us to do in in order to receive really good things from him:
* Seek him
* Wait for him
* Trust him

Do these 3 things daily in all their fullness and you can expect God to give you good things to help you thrive and do well in life, just like the Israelites and the many other believers in the Bible.

How do we learn to *trust* God? → By really getting to know him. That will only happen if we seek him out of a hunger to experience him. **If you're *not* hungry for God**, you probably won't seek to know him. And if you don't know him very well, you probably won't really *trust* him that much. And if you don't trust him for good things, you probably won't receive them.

Most of us will trust someone with the important things in our lives if we really know them well. Trust is won, not given. Has God won your trust? The only way we're going to truly trust God with the important things in our lives is to get to know him, intimately. And that will only happen when we diligently, carefully, and consistently seek to know him.

You might be wondering → *Well how does that work? How should I seek him?*
Here's the answer:
* Diligently = to apply effort, to work at it with attention and persistence. It's not a casual thing.

* <u>Consistently</u> = not sporadically for 15 minutes here and 10 minutes there. Make it regular and organized. Discipline yourself.

* <u>Carefully</u> = the word means 'full-of-care'. It doesn't mean to randomly open your Bible and point to any verse, or turn on YouTube and watch any sermon that just shows up (although I do believe God can use those methods to reach us). It means to put some thought into it, to use some care when seeking him.

<u>Mybe you're thinking</u> → *"Well, I try to seek him, but he just seems so far away. It feels impossible to know him."*
Here's the answer:

<u>Deuteronomy 4:29</u> → *If you seek God with <u>all</u> your heart* (diligently, carefully, and consistently, out of hunger to know him), *you <u>will</u> find him and come to know him.*

That's a guarantee. It doesn't say you *'may'* find him. No, it says you *'will'* find him, as long as you seek him with <u>all</u> your heart. Yeah, it takes effort...but that's the way it is. So, seek him.

"All things are difficult before they are easy." — *Thomas Fuller*

<u>Plus</u>, God says that he'll *reward* you for it.

<u>Hebrews 11:6</u> → *God <u>rewards</u> those who <u>diligently</u> seek him.*

What's the <u>reward</u>? I'm not sure, but it must be good because a reward from God is *always* good.

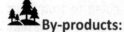**By-products:**
Hey, did you know that <u>happiness</u> is a by-product of trusting God? Check it out.

<u>Psalm 40:4</u> says → *There is <u>happiness</u> for those who <u>trust</u> the Lord.*

If this promise is true, then our hearts should be happy as a result of trusting God, right? How would that look in our lives? I would probably say that inner happiness and contentment is a good description. **Why?** Because when we take the load off our shoulders and put it on God, trusting him to carry our burdens, we feel lighter, happier, and even content, knowing we don't have to worry about it anymore.

Here's another by-product of trusting God → Strength

⊕ Isaiah 40:31 → *Those who put their <u>trust in the Lord</u> and <u>wait for him to act</u> will <u>renew their strength</u>. They will soar like an eagle and run without getting tired.*

The Hebrew meaning for the phrase '*<u>wait for him to act</u>*' infers patience and resting, not trying to do something on our own to fix the situation we're in. The way to renew our strength is to *rest...not 'do'.*

The phrase '*<u>renew their strength</u>*'in Hebrew means '<u>to make</u> <u>strong *again*</u>'. Do you remember times in your life when you felt strong, when you felt on top of the world, that nothing could knock you down? That's the meaning behind '*<u>renew</u>*' in this verse. You're back on top. You're on your A-game once again. **How's that gonna happen?** By letting go and trusting God with everything in your life – the good, the bad, and the ugly; and then resting and waiting with expectation for him to come through.
What will the result be? The burden will be lifted. You'll feel like you could soar like an eagle, like you could run a marathon and not get tired. You get the idea, right?

So, what should we do to feel strong and on top of the world again? → 2 things. <u>Trust</u> God and <u>Wait</u> for him to act. You'll know you're doing it because you'll feel renewed, not tired or wasted, but ready to soar and ready to run the race.

🌲🌲**Wanna know how God wants us to live?**

⊕ Galatians 2:20 → *It is no longer just me living my life, but Christ is living within me, and the life I now live in this earthly body of mine, I live by <u>faith</u>, by <u>trusting</u> in Christ, the son of God...*

Question: Are you living your life, just tolerating, and putting up with whatever comes your way? Or...are you mixing <u>faith</u> and <u>trust</u> into the little and big things that happen to you throughout your day, directing your attention to God, inviting him into the middle of it all, and expecting him to do great things?

I can tell you that once I started doing that, life became much more exciting. I began seeing amazing things happen to me that I can only attribute to God. It's actually fun to let go of the reins and sit back to watch God move on your behalf. When you think about it, that's what faith is all about, right?

Faith talks in the language of God.

We all know that to become prolific in any language it takes practice, practice, practice, until it becomes natural.

The thing is, when we first come to God, we're usually walking and talking the world's language, not God's language. After all, that's all we've known. Then God starts to teach us his language...the language of faith, because he knows without faith it's impossible to live the new life he gives us.

Jesus had to _learn_ the language of faith as well. He walked out his earthly life depending completely on God, just the same as we are called to do. In fact, he said, *'I can do nothing on my own. I depend on what I hear from God to make my judgments, and my decisions are right because I obey God's will, not my own.'* (See John 5:30)

So, if we're going to learn to trust God with all those guarantees he offers us in his promises, then we better learn to speak God's language...<u>the language of faith</u>.

To trust God in the light of understanding takes little effort, but to trust him in the darkness of the unknowing? – well that's faith.

HELP FROM GOD
What God promises

We all need God to help us in our troubles...but also to help us in our blessings. Anonymous

Not all of us are in desperate need of God's help right at the moment, but all of us need his help at some point in time.
So, what does God say about helping us?

I think this needs to be said first: Sometimes, I think our tendency is to talk more about our problems than we need to. Maybe you've heard it said: *Instead of talking about how big our problems are, we need to talk about how big our God is.* I believe that, how about you? But, do we really do it? If we do, then the next three verses should be a vital part of our lives.

How big is God's ability to help you?

Here are three quick <u>promises</u>:

Luke 1:37 → *With God, <u>nothing</u> is impossible.*

Mathew19:26 Jesus speaking → *With man it may be impossible, but with God <u>all</u> things are possible.*

Genesis 18:14 → *Is <u>anything</u> too hard for God?*

Do you know what's linked to all three of those verses? Good things. God's intention behind saying those statements was to bless the reader/listener with newfound confidence in him and that's exactly what happened. We should expect the same thing. They are universal truths in the Bible and therefore they are promises we can claim for our own lives.

Those three promises are pretty easy to memorize and once you know them by heart, it's easy to **ABC** them.

And just to remind you: **ABC** stands for → **A**gree with God that nothing's impossible for him...**B**elieve it in your heart that this applies to your life...**C**onfess it (in your heart or out loud) over and over again to feed your faith and starve your doubt.

If you want God's help, then first learn to _'throw'_.

1 Peter 5:7 → _Cast_ (Greek meaning - **throw**) _all of your cares_ (all of your worries, concerns, anxieties, and fears) _onto God. For he cares about you deeply because you profoundly matter to him._

What does it say we should do? → **Throw**, literally throw all that stuff that's bothering us off of ourselves and onto God. Why? Because he cares enough about us to not let us carry all of that stuff alone. Throwing is aggressive and it takes effort, but that's what we have to do if we want God to help us. We can't carry it all alone. So, don't.

By the way, it doesn't say to throw those burdens onto friends, or loved ones (as good as their advice might be). It doesn't say to throw them onto a therapist (as much as they may help us), and it doesn't say to just give them over to fate or anything else. No...God is specifically saying to throw them onto him. Don't forget, God has all the right answers to our problems. So, throw those worries and burdens onto him.

Think about this for a moment → If you've thrown your worries and fears onto God, then, guess what? You're no longer carrying them. He is. So, look at your hands, your shoulders, your back. Are you carrying anything? Hopefully not. You should feel lighter. You're burden-free. God's carrying the load for you.

Remember this → God never ever intended you to carry your burdens by yourself. So, don't. Do some _throwing_.

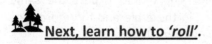Next, learn how to _'roll'_.

Psalm 37:5 → *Commit everything you do to the Lord.* (the Hebrew meaning is to **roll** each one of your cares and concerns <u>off</u> of you and <u>onto</u> God). *Trust him with them <u>all</u> and then he will <u>help</u> you.* (Hebrew meaning – <u>He will work it all out for you.</u> He will attend to it and put it all in order)

Do you really want God's help? Then do those <u>2 things</u>.
1) <u>Roll</u> those worries and concerns onto him...and only him. If you do, then you're no longer carrying your worries.
2) <u>Entrust</u> them to him. (Completely let go...and let God)

It's one thing to *<u>roll</u>* those burdens onto God. It's another thing to *<u>leave</u>* them there, entrusted to his care, not taking them back.

But, if you do *both* of those steps, then God will work it *<u>all</u>* out for you. He guarantees it. God will make it *all* work out *for you*...for *you*! That means he cares enough about *you* to zero in on your life and work out all the details of your problem. When you think about it, that's amazing! You really, truly matter to him. God doesn't *have* to help you. He *wants* to. Trusting him just makes him want to help even more.

 Next, be _'certain'_.

Romans 8:28 → *We know* (Greek meaning -- to be convinced with certainty) *that if we love God, he will cause each and every detail of our lives to work together* (blended and woven together) *so that it turns out in the end for our good.*

Here's a question for you: Are you convinced and <u>certain of this guarantee</u>? Do you believe that God can take your crummy situation and turn it into good, even if it's not what you were hoping for? If not, then why not? It's ok to question ourselves about these things. It's what makes our faith become real.

Sometimes I think it would be easier to just simply believe than doubt. Afterall, the difference between the two is simply a <u>choice</u> ...nothing more. So, **MAC** it→ **M**ake **A C**hoice...to believe.

By the way, you probably already know this, but for those who need to hear it again.→ When that promise says that God will work it all out <u>for our good</u>, the end-result may different than what we want or expect. Right? We have to look at it through God's lens, not our own. God might have something completely different in mind for us. But what we can definitely hang our hat on is this → It will always benefit us. We win, because God's always good to us...always.

Here's another promise about God's help:

<u>Isaiah 41:10</u> God speaking → *Don't be anxious or worried or afraid, for I (God) am with you. And don't be discouraged about your circumstances, for I am your God. I will <u>strengthen</u> you* (Hebrew meaning - make you stronger and support you) *and I will <u>help</u> you* (Hebrew meaning - come to your aid, protect you, and provide for you), *and I will <u>hold you up</u> by my right hand.*

Every one of those guarantees mentioned in that promise are meant as a blessing for us. Again, why would God even bother to do those things for us? It's because he cares about us deeply in his heart and wants to make our lives easier. Remember that fact when you're tempted to think he doesn't care about you.

So, what are the guarantees in that verse? → 5 of them.
1.) God says <u>he'll be *with* us</u>. My question is this.→ Is there anyone greater in this universe other than God who could be with us? Not that I know of. How 'bout you? So, don't look elsewhere. If God's saying he's with us, why doubt it?

2.) He says <u>he's *our* God</u>. That means he isn't a statue in a church. He's alive and personal, and he wants to be intimately involved in our lives...*if* we'll let him.

3.) He says <u>he'll make us stronger</u>. In what way? → physically stronger, emotionally stronger, and spiritually stronger. What area do you need strength in? He'll strengthen you in that area.

4.) He says <u>he'll help us</u>. How? → Any way he wants to. That's up to him. Just know it will happen and it will be for our good.

5.) He says he'll <u>hold us up with his right hand of victory</u>. → In the Old Testament, when kings held up their right hand in battle, it was a sign of victory...that the battle is being won. And here's the thing we need to continually remember.→ God is always victorious...I mean *always*. So, guess what? We'll be victorious as well. In other words, we won't lose. So, believe it.

My question is this → If he's our father in heaven, the creator of the universe, is there anything too hard for him?

So, what are we worried about? If God is for us, then who can overcome us?

Let's make it personal → What is God telling *you* to do, in that verse? That's right. Don't allow *yourself* to be worried, anxious, or afraid. Don't talk about how huge your problem is, talk about how huge God is...that he's right beside *you*, that he's making *you* stronger, that he's helping *you*, that he's giving *you* the victory. **Talk about that**. Tell God, tell yourself, and tell others.

Sidenote → Many promise-verses in this book can be applied to other areas of our life. To give you an example, look at this next promise covered in the section on Trouble:

Psalm 46:1 → *God is my* refuge (Hebrew meaning - In his presence is safety, rest, and peace). *And God is my strength* (His strength becomes my strength, emotionally, physically, and spiritually). *In fact, he is always ready to jump in and **help** me in times of trouble and distress*.

This promise can apply when we're going through trouble and need God's help, or it can apply when we need a refuge and a place of rest from the stresses of life. Either way, it's a promise and it's there for us to use it. So, speak it to yourself with faith.

Do you feel that God isn't listening to you? He is. He says in that promise that he's *always* ready to help you. How can he *always* be ready to help you if he's *not* paying close attention to your circumstances? Do you believe it? That's the question. If you truly believe it, then what are you going to do with that promise? Are you going to make him your refuge and strength?

You might be thinking → *"I just feel like I'm talking to a brick wall when I ask God for help."*

My Answer→ It could be a 'waiting' thing. Or it could be that he *is* answering you and you're just not seeing it. I can't tell you how many times that was my case. Or it could be something that needs changing in your life before God acts. I think we need to do a 'self-check' on our lives several times a week, just to see if we're missing anything God wants to change in us? **Here is a great way to do a 'self-check'**. Read the verse below:

✦ **Psalm 139:23,24** → *Search me, God, to know what's in my heart. Examine me, to know what my thoughts are. Point out to me anything that you may want to change in me, and then lead me along the godly path of everlasting life.*

This is where it helps to use what God says in his Word as a measuring stick on our lives, to see if we're doing what he says. After all, if we want his help, then it would be good to know what he expects from us to make it happen. Here's an example of what I mean:

✦ **1 Peter 3:12** → *God notices and pays attention to those who continually do what is right before him. And, because of this, his ears are attentive to their prayers.*

We might claim that verse as a promise, but we *also* might use it as a 'measuring stick' → Are we continually doing what's right before his eyes? Pretty important to know if we want God to listen to our prayers, don't you think?

Too many of us think that God is supposed to automatically hear us when we pray. But that's not always the case according to that verse.

Wanna know how to guarantee that God _will_ hear your prayers? → Just as that verse says - continually make the choice to live as he tells you to, doing what's right before his eyes. If you do, he guarantees he'll pay attention to your prayers.

Wanna know a good way for God _not_ to hear your prayers? That's right. → continually *don't* do what's right before his eyes.

Here's a verse to help us continually choose to do what's right:
I call it **The Crossroad Verse**.

✦ **Jeremiah 6:16** → *When you come to a crossroad in your life, stop* (don't go any further, don't turn left or right or even go straight ahead), *and then <u>look</u> around* (understand where you're at...your heart, your intentions, and your motives). *Then <u>ask</u> for the godly way and walk in it. <u>Travel</u> its path and you'll find true <u>rest</u> and peace. But, what's your response? You <u>refuse</u>, saying, "No thanks. I'm not going that way. I'm going the way I want."*

There's so much wisdom in this verse on how to make the right choices. If you apply it to your life, you can't go wrong.

There are <u>7 important points in that verse</u>, and here they are:
1) <u>Stop</u> → When you reach a crossroad in your life where you have to decide how you're going to proceed...<u>stop</u>. Don't turn to the left or the right or go any further. Do the next step.
2)<u>Look</u> → Look around. Understand where you're at...your heart, your intentions, your motives. Are they aligned with God?
3) <u>Ask</u> → Ask God for the right way to go.
4) <u>Travel</u> → When you get the answer, <u>travel</u> down that path.
5) <u>Rest</u> → Check to see if you're at <u>rest</u> in your heart and have peace about the decision you've made. (Too many of us make decisions without checking for *peace*)
6) <u>Don't Refuse</u> → Don't say, *"No thanks. I'm not going that way. I'm going the way I want."*
7) <u>Repeat</u> → Practice these steps until they're a regular part of your life. It will keep you out of a world of trouble.

Saint Augustine said: *"O Lord, help me to be pure, just not yet."*

Isn't that just the way we are? Oh, you're not? Huh, then I guess maybe it's just me.☺ But, seriously though, if we just lived by this **Crossroads Verse**, we'd make our lives soooo much easier.

One more promise:

Isaiah 41:13 → *I, the Lord Your God, am the one who <u>holds your right hand</u>, and I say to you, 'Don't be anxious or afraid, I am here to <u>help</u> you.'*

I think when God speaks, we sometimes don't take him very seriously. When God says he's holding our hand, do we believe it? Imagine what it would feel like. Do you remember what when you held someone's hand and It felt safe, strong, and comforting? If God's holding our hand, shouldn't it feel the same way? When he offers his hand to you...take it.

When God says not to worry or be afraid _because_ he's holding our hand and he's here to help us, then we need to take him at his word, and *stop* our worrying and fear. It's simple when you think about it.

You know why God spoke those words? Because he wanted us to know he's right there with us, and whether it feels like it or not, he's still there holding our hand. We just have to trust what he's saying. Imagine holding God's hand and us insisting on being worried, anxious, and afraid. That wouldn't work, right?

And don't forget that God is declaring that he's holding your _right_ hand. Let me repeat what I mentioned a few pages back: When kings in the Old Testament held up their right hand in battle, it was a sign of victory...that the battle is being won. And here's the thing we need to continually remember.→ God is _always_ victorious...I mean '*always*'. So, guess what? We'll be victorious as well. In other words, we won't lose. So, believe it.

Want some _help_ from God? Well, he's holding out his hand. All you have to do is take it. He'll lift it up as sign for all to see that the battle is being won! And what do you suppose the outcome will be for you? – Victory! All we have to do is not let go, right?

It may not always feel like a victory, but if you make sure to see it through God's lens, you'll begin to see the *good* in the bad stuff that happens to you. Can there actually be any good in the rotten stuff that happens to us? It's all a matter of which perspective we choose to take. For example, Jesus' torturous death on the cross may not have seemed like much of a victory, but it was a gigantic triumph...through the lens of God. It only becomes a victory for us when we see it the way God sees it. That's why it's important to see most of the things in our lives from God's perspective. He sees the lemonade, not the lemons. What do you see?

No matter what you face in your life, take God's hand and never let go.

STRENGTH
God Promises To Give Us Strength

I love this quote from Ernest Hemingway: *"The world breaks everyone, and afterward, some are strong at the broken places."*

That's it, isn't it? We need to be strong in *our* broken places. Only God can make that happen.

For many people, just surviving each day can be consuming to them. For others, trials and adversities rob them of strength. And, still, others do ok, but by the end of the day or week, they feel like they've been beaten up.

So, What Does God Guarantee Us About Strength?

Did you know that God is looking for you?

It says so right here:

2 Chronicles 16:9 → *God continually searches the whole earth in order to strengthen* (Hebrew meaning – to make strong, to strongly support, and to enable to prevail) *those whose hearts are fully committed to him* (Hebrew meaning– those who have given themselves completely to him, whose hearts are completely his). *He wants to strengthen them.*

It seems hard to believe sometimes that God can be everywhere, know everything, and hear all our prayers, all at the same time. I mean, how big is God anyway? Can he permeate the whole earth all at once with his Spirit? It takes faith to grasp that, doesn't it? However, it becomes easier when we remove the humanistic restrictions and features we place on God and just trust that *if* he has the ability to create the intricacies of the universe that extend from galaxies billions of light-years away all the way down to our DNA, then he's certainly able to do what he says in that promise.

And think about this: Why would God even bother to search the earth for people who have a heart for him just so he could strengthen them? It's because he loves us so deeply that it's important to him to search. That's amazing, isn't it?

You know what that promise has attached to it? - A contingency. → We have to have a heart that's completely given to God. If that's you, then God's looking for you in order to personally strengthen you and support you.

So, if you want **guaranteed strength** from God, then make sure your heart is in the right place, and then remind God of his promise.

🌲🌲**Remember this amazing guarantee?**

✦ **Isaiah 41:10** → _Don't_ _worry or be troubled, anxious, or afraid about anything, for I, God, am with you_ (there is no one greater in the entire universe who could be with you).

And don't be discouraged about the situation you're in, for I am your God (I deeply care about you. I am personally involved in your life. And for me, nothing is too difficult.)

If you refuse to worry or be discouraged and you put your trust in me, I will do the following for you:

• _I will personally_ **_strengthen_** _you_ (meaning, I will make you stronger emotionally, physically, and spiritually).

• _And I will help you_ (meaning I will come to your aid and protect you).

• _I will hold you up with my victorious right hand_ (meaning, you'll be victorious because I am always victorious... you won't fight the battle alone).

Where in this promise does it leave any room for worries, anxiety, fear, or discouragement? As far as I can see, absolutely nowhere. I mean, here's the highest being in the universe – God, our own creator, who's telling us there's no reason to be worried or afraid...that he's personally right there in the battle with us and that he's offering to strengthen us, and help us, and give us victory. Who wouldn't want that? It's like having the biggest, baddest, strongest life coach, personal trainer, and bodyguard all rolled into one.

Here's the thing we need to grasp: Before we can receive his strength, his help, and his victory, we need to make a choice. What's the choice? That we _won't allow_ ourselves to be worried, we won't allow ourselves to be troubled, or anxious or afraid.

Why is that important? Because those feelings are the opposite of faith. They can't coexist with our faith. We have to push them aside and not allow them to creep back in. When faith is leading the way, then God can step in to give us his supernatural strength, his help us and his victory. So, make the choice → MAC it.

You know what? I find it helpful in my own life to remind God of what he said he'd do. I know God doesn't need to be reminded, but it helps me stay in 'faith-mode'. It feeds my faith and starves my doubt. Try it yourself. Remind him. He likes it when we do.

Are you feeling drained of energy and strength? It's hard to put the effort out to follow God when we feel that way, isn't it? God understands and he feels what we feel. He promises he'll empower us during those times.

Isaiah 40:29 → _God gives strength to those who feel tired and worn-out. And he gives power to those who feel powerless._

There are two things we must pull from that verse:

1.) There's no reason we have to remain in that spiritually worn-out or powerless state. Why? Because the source of strength and power mentioned in that verse is coming from God, not us. It says _he_ is the one giving it. It's supernaturally coming from him.

2.) That promise is a guarantee, and we need to treat it that way. God will not allow his kids who are spiritually exhausted to remain like that. He'll jump in to help, to give us the strength we need to face whatever we're going through. But it won't become real in our lives unless we receive it. And we can't receive it until we step out in faith and believe what God says he will do. So, what are you going to do with that verse?

And how does God even know when we need <u>strength</u>? Is it only when we ask him? Or could it be that he also has his eye personally on us, that he's paying attention to us, and is intimately aware of the details of our lives.

God wants us weak!

<u>2 Corinthians 12:9</u> → *My grace is <u>all you need</u>. In fact, my power <u>always works best</u> in a person's weakness.*

<u>You might be thinking</u> → *"Wait a second! I thought God wanted us strong. Now you're saying he wants us weak? Which is it???"*

Here's the thing → When we finally *stop* trying to do things in our own strength, and get out of the way to let God strengthen us with *his* power to do it his way, that's when we make way for a <u>supernatural outcome</u>.

Think about that for a second → If God's power were being displayed in our <u>weakest</u> moments, what might that look like? Shouldn't it look *supernatural*? I mean, if God's power is supernatural, then shouldn't we see a supernatural outcome? I think so. How about you?

But you know what might be the hardest thing to do? <u>Waiting!</u>...waiting to see that supernatural outcome; waiting for God to show up with his supernatural power...especially when we feel weak and on a losing streak.

Here's what God guarantees us: We've covered this one before:

<u>Isaiah 40:31</u> → Those *who* ***wait patiently*** *for God, trusting him to help them; they <u>will renew their strength</u>* (their strength will be made new again). *They will rise up and fly like an eagle. They will run and not get tired.*

The strength being renewed here is *our* strength, not God's strength. We've been talking about God infusing *his* strength into us, but in this promise, it's talking about us regaining our own strength. That will only happen when we relax, rest, stop trying, and start trusting...just <u>waiting</u> for God to act.

Too often we're impatient for God to work out the situation for us, so we start doing stuff on our own to fix it...the complete opposite of resting and *waiting*. All that does is wear us out.

Waiting on God means he does the work, and we **rest**. Resting renews our strength, renews our faith, renews our confidence, so we can rise up and fly high above our circumstances, so we can run the distance. God renews our strength, but we do it too by resting.

Just remember → Noah waited 120 years before God did what he said he'd do -- bring the rains and flood. And Abraham waited 25 years for the son God promised him. And Joseph waited 14 years in prison for God to deliver him from a crime he didn't even commit. All of them trusted God and waited for him to act.

God sometimes produces patience and endurance in us by putting us in a slow-pressure-cooker. I think we want the *microwave*. But, what's most important of all is the work God accomplishes within us *while* we're doing the waiting.

Look at this instructional verse:

1 Chronicle 16:11 → *Search for God and seek his strength. In fact, seek his face continually* (throughout our lives).

Part of waiting on God is resting, as I just mentioned. And part of resting is seeking God as well as seeking *his* strength. It's interesting that it doesn't say for us to seek ways to make *ourselves* stronger. I sometimes think there are too many self-help books and social media videos that we rely on to empower us rather than getting our strength from God. That verse says to seek *his* strength, and as a result, *his* strength becomes *our* strength. That's the way we should be living – in his strength.

Bottom-line: We can gather from the last two verses the following:
1) If we *rest* and *wait* on God (not doing things to fix it ourselves), it will renew us *physically* and make us *emotionally* stronger.

2) If we <u>seek</u> his face and his strength *while* we're resting and waiting on him, we'll become stron
ger *spiritually.*

And, you know what? He knows <u>exactly how much strength</u> to give us. He doesn't just dish out a random amount to everyone. No, he's aware of our own situation and he gives us just the right type of strength and the right amount he knows we need.

Seeking strength from God won't be easy if God is a stranger to us; if he's just some entity we pray to *only when* we need help during our troubles. We're only as close to God as we want to be. He's never far away. It's us who stay away. Too often, we're so busy with the distractions of life, seeking him becomes hard and uncomfortable when in fact it should be easy.

 You know what I think? We've become God's family of *'maintenance people'*. We're so busy maintaining our lives, our home, our family, our yard, our cars, our work, etc. that we don't have any time left to maintain our relationship with God. We don't have the time to seek him and the strength he offers. But can we spiritually afford to do that? I don't think so.

That verse is telling us where to go for strength, and if we go to God for it, we'll be empowered with *his* personal supernatural strength, above and beyond our own. <u>The only thing that could keep that from happening</u> is our own unwillingness. Don't let that happen to you. **Seek God and be empowered by him.**

God wants <u>his</u> strength to be <u>our</u> strength:

Ephesians 6:10 → *Be strong <u>in</u> the Lord* (meaning receive strength from him, live by his strength, make his strength your strength) *and be empowered with <u>his</u> power.*

God wants to give us his <u>personal</u> strength, his personal power. He makes that very clear over and over again through his Word. Either we're receiving supernatural strength from God or we're managing the situations in our lives in our own strength. Either we get up each day and live out the day empowered by God, or we don't. **Which is it for you?** I mean, if God is your co-pilot, then switch seats. He should be captain.

You might be wondering → *"I still don't get it. How do I receive his strength or his power?"*

Here's my answer → We open our hands, our hearts, our minds and just take it in by faith. Receiving strength from God is not because we *'will'* it to happen. It's trusting God to give it to us. We should be walking through each day empowered by his strength. It should be a supernatural, everyday normal occurrence for us, don't you think? Nothing weird, just normal.

And keep this in mind → We can't fight our battles in our own strength. Too many of us do that. It has to be his strength in us. How on earth do we do that?

✥ **Zechariah 4:6** → *It's not going to happen by your own strength, nor by any other power, but it will happen by my Spirit, says the Lord.*

And read this promise:

✥ *Ephesians 3:16* → *God will empower you with miraculous inner strength through his Spirit (living within you).*

That's how we do it...God's strength becomes our strength *by way of* the His Spirit within us.

God's strength is a distinct spiritual force apart from our own strength, and it flows within us by way of his Spirit. It's a supernatural result of the Holy Spirit residing in us, giving us *his* supernatural power.

We should be able to feel it, right? I mean, if God's strength is flowing within us, then it should feel different from our own strength, shouldn't it? If that's so, then we should look for it, expecting to feel it, expecting it to affect the outcome of the situations in our lives. If we're going to live spiritual lives, then we need do spiritual things. Receiving God's strength through his Spirit is a spiritual thing. It's part of living by faith.

You might be thinking → *"That sounds like spiritual hocus-pocus! I need real strength, not some spiritual make-believe."*

I get it, it does sound kind of weird. But you know what? In God's world, it's normal. And he called us to live in his world. All the great men and women of the Bible accomplished great things only through God's strength flowing through them by faith. It was normal for them, and it should be *normal* for us.

So you want real strength? It's going to take faith. *Faith* is what opens the door for God's supernatural strength to operate in us by way of his Spirit. Without faith, we're simply operating in our own human strength. When we leave out faith, we leave out the supernatural aspect of our life with God. Let's not do that. Let's use our faith to receive God's strength so we can live and operate in the supernatural realm of God's world.

You know what? In order for those last two promises to come true in your own life, you'll have to decide whether you'll believe them...or not. Faith is a choice. Are you going to believe God will empower you with mighty inner strength through his Spirit? If yes, then ask for it, wait for it, watch for it, feel it.

By the way, the word '*empower*' in that last verse is the Greek word '*dynamis*' which is where we get the word '*dynamite*'. It means to infuse with '*miraculous forceful power*'.

In other words, the inner strength from God we're talking about is not '*just enough*' strength to barely make it through. Nope, it's mighty and miraculous strength infused with power. That's the kind of strength we want, isn't it? And it only comes by his Spirit.

 So, it's not just, "*God, give me strength.*" No, it's, "*God, you promised that your Spirit living in me will give me mighty, powerful inner strength. And I know that not one single word of all your promises has ever failed. So, here I am. Give it to me! I wanna feel it. I want to see the difference. I'll wait, cause I'm expecting you to come through, just like you promised.*"

Shouldn't we be able to feel God's Spirit within us as well?
Most of the time I would say, no, but sometimes, yes. God's Spirit is not physical but spiritual in substance, so we have to think of it in spiritual terms. We can feel his nudges, his conviction, and hear his small whispers. We can sense God's truth being revealed to us as he teaches us from his Word. We

can feel him operating in us through the various gifts God's given us, and we can feel him strengthening us physically, emotionally, and spiritually.

You might be mumbling to yourself → *"Man, you sound like one of those religious nuts."*

I get it. I've heard it said: *"God wants spiritual 'fruit', not religious 'nuts'."* But is it really that strange to think that we're spirits with a soul, living in a physical body? The Bible says it's our spirit that God makes alive, and it's our spirit that lives on after our bodies die. I mean, think about it, we can't see the air, yet without it we're physically dead, so it is with the Holy Spirit – we can't see him, yet without him we're spiritually dead.

Now read these two verses about God's Spirit living in you:

1 Corinthians 6:19 → *Do you not know that you are the temple of the Holy Spirit, whom God gave you and <u>who lives within you</u>?*b

Romans 8:9 → *You're no longer dominated by your sin-bent flesh, but now you're led by the Holy Spirit, <u>who lives in you</u>.*

Ok, so let's get real here → Do you really believe that God's Holy Spirit lives within you? It's a *'yes'* or *'no'* answer...not *'maybe'*. Because if you don't, then how do you expect God to empower you with inner strength through his Spirit? It's not going to happen without faith involved.

Perhaps you're thinking → *"I just don't feel God's Spirit in me. Not at all! Is something wrong with me?"*

Nope. It takes faith to believe it as fact...but here's the thing. We know God doesn't lie. If he says his Spirit lives in us, then we just need to believe it. He's God and we're not. So, believe it.

"But still...aren't I supposed to feel something...anything?"
Let me ask you something. Can you feel your blood flowing throughout your body? No. But you know that it's happening, otherwise, you'd be dead. You kind of accept it by faith. Right?

It's the same for God's Spirit. He's living in you with his spiritual life flowing through you. It's what makes you spiritually alive. Without him, you'd be spiritually dead (Do you remember what that felt like?) And, just as you accept the fact that your blood flows through you making you alive physically, just accept by faith that God's Spirit flows through you making you alive spiritually.

And, get this → Jesus said to a man who brought his child to be healed: *"Anything is possible if a person will just believe."* You know what the father of the child's response was? *"I do believe, Lord. I do. But help me overcome my unbelief."*

Don't be afraid to tell God the same thing. Notice the man asked Jesus for help with his unbelief. And that's what Jesus did. God is more than happy to do the same for you if you ask him.

God wants nothing but good things for you. So, tell him what you're feeling. He'll be glad you're being honest. He knows your heart anyway. He won't hold it against you. He wants to help. So, tell him. I dare ya.

Hey, I have to include this fabulous guarantee:

2 Thessalonians 3:3 → *God is always faithful* (he's always true to his word and always does what he says he'll do), *He will strengthen you and protect you from evil* (or the evil-one).

Has God ever been unfaithful to you? Ever? Because, if he's *only* been faithful to you, then he'll do what he says he'll do – he'll strengthen you. But it's up to you to *believe* he'll do it. He's willing and ready. He's just waiting for you to believe. He wants his kid's strong, not weak...protected, not vulnerable to harm. Believing will unlock the door for that to happen.

The Greek word for 'strengthen' in that verse means to make you so strong that you're firmly fixed in place, immovable. Nothing's going to shake you because you're unfaltering and unbendable. Evil can't knock you down cause you're strong and protected. That's the kind of strength God wants to give you.

Notice there are two aspects of God's strength involved in that promise – One is *within* us (God is strengthening us from the enemy's inward attacks, like emotional hurt, pain, and doubt) and the other is _outside_ us (God using his strength to protect us from evil that could harm us).

🌲 Here's a point we need to remember:

The battles we go through are not for us to fight *alone*. We must let God into the struggle. If we do that, our strength and protection from the evil-one will come from God. Look at this next promise:

🧭 **Deuteronomy 20:4** → *God goes with you, to fight for you on your behalf and he will give you the victory against your enemies.*

God always wants to be right in the middle of our struggles...right smack in the middle. He wants us to win every single battle...every one of them. He knows that won't happen without *his* strength and protection. Don't go into the fight without them.

🌲 Now, what's all this about battling *"the evil-one"*?

Ok, this is a thorny subject, but here goes: Would you agree that it seems evil is all around us? It has one source...the enemies of our soul. Even though we're fighting the battles of our lives in the three dimensions of the 'here and now', we can't forget it's also in the spiritual realm as well.

Take a look at this verse:

🧭 **Ephesians 6:12** → *Our fight* (our struggles in this life) *is not really with human beings, but rather it's against evil rulers and powerful forces of darkness in the spiritual realm.*

And this verse:

🧭 **1 Peter 5:8** → *Watch out and be on the alert because your enemy, the devil, is just like a roaring lion who is ferociously hungry and searching for someone to devour.*

Are you watching out? Are you on the alert, or is the word *'devil'* an obscure concept that's just too creepy for you?

There's no shame in thinking that, but we still need to realize that our problems may be more than just what we see on the surface. They most likely have a spiritual component as well.

Speaking of a *'spiritual component'*, do you know what's interesting? In the Old Testament, kings warred against other kings, and yet it was God who often said that _he_ was the one leading one nation into battle against the other and that he was arranging for one side to beat the other.

So, these kings and nations were going to war, making their own battle decisions, and fighting the battles themselves physically, yet behind the scenes, in the spiritual realm, God was making stuff happen...sort of rearranging the chess board, so to speak.

The point is this: There seems to be two sides to the situations in our lives...one side is this tangible life, and the other side (invisible to us) is the spiritual.

So, going back to this stuff about evil, just a little bit more.

If we want to win the battles we go through in our lives, then we need to make sure we're *surrendered* to God (letting go of controlling the situation, and getting out of the way so he can move on our behalf). It also means we'll need to pick up the weapons God gives us to resist the evil-one's attacks. Part of being strengthened by God is using his weapons of choice against our enemy. Here are three verses about the spiritual side of the battles we go through.

James 4:7 → *Surrender yourselves to God. Then, resist (fight) against the evil-one and he will flee from you.*

<u>SIDENOTE</u>:

- The meaning of the word **'_surrender_'** in Greek, is *to relinquish control and submit yourself under the authority and rulership of another.* → In our case, that's God.

- The meaning of the word **'_resist_'** in Greek, is *to set yourself against, to fight against.* → Are you fighting back?

- The meaning of the word **'_flee_'** in Greek, is *to vanish, to run away from something abhorrent.* → The enemy will flee.

When we surrender ourselves to God, we relinquish control over our <u>lives</u>...not our will, our lives. We surrender to God as our king, and we allow him to rule over our lives. It also means we stop doing things in our own strength and start using the strength God offers us. We let him into the battle so he can fight along-side us.

Well, if the evil-one is so powerful, then why would he <u>flee</u> from measly little you?
Because you've surrendered your *'self'* (what self wants) to God's will (what God wants), and the evil-one has less influence on you now. It doesn't mean he won't try to tempt you, but because you've surrendered yourself to God, it means you're no longer surrendering to the whims of your *'self'* or the influence of the enemy. Now God's power can shine through you and the enemy will flee. That's what that verse means by *'resisting'* the evil one.

Here are two more verses that will help us:

Ephesians 4:27 → *Don't give the evil-one the <u>opportunity</u>* (don't make it easy for him) *to defeat you*.

The key word there is **"<u>opportunity</u>"**, which in this verse, means making yourself available to the influences of evil-one.

Ephesians 6:11 → *Put on (wear) <u>all</u> of God's armor **so that** you will be protected and be able to <u>fight</u> against the devil's schemes and tricks*.

Those two underlined words "<u>so that</u>" are important. It means, *'you have to do a specific thing <u>so that</u> you'll get a specific result'*. In other words, if you want to be successful in your fight against the schemes of the enemy in your life, then you have to <u>put on</u> God's armor...all of it, <u>so that</u> you'll be protected. Don't store it in your spiritual closet. Wear it.

Too many of us get clobbered by the enemy because we don't have the protection we need to be able withstand the attacks. That makes us weak not strong. But God has given us exactly what we need to wear. Just like wearing a Kevlar vest, how much more confident would we be in the fight if we were wearing protection? (Ephesians 6:14-17 describes the pieces of the amor we should wear.) Too many of us leave the armor at home when we go about our day. Then when we get attacked, we're unprepared. So, put it on. Lucky for us, God's armor isn't heavy. It's spiritual armor. It's part of the strength God gives us. **Remember, if we want to live spiritual lives, then we have to do spiritual things.** → Slip it on.

<u>**When we put the last 3 verses together, there are 4 things we need to do**</u>:

1. <u>Surrender</u> to God (Surrender our *'self'* to what God wants for us, not what *'self'* wants)

2. <u>Resist</u> (put up a fight) against the enemy. Don't whimp-out.

3. Don't give the devil the <u>opportunity</u> to mislead you. Don't even get near the line of temptation, let alone cross it.

4. <u>Wear</u> *all* of God's <u>armor</u>. (To know more about God's armor read Ephesians 6, starting at verse 11)

You might be thinking → *"All this talk about the devil. That's way too creepy for me!"*

I get it. It's creepy for me too. But guess who talked about the devil more than anyone else? Jesus. And right behind him were the Apostles Paul, Peter, John, and James. They all treated the devil as real, so we should do the same. Writing off the 'evil-one' and his minions as if they don't exist is like wading into shark-infested waters and ignoring the warning signs on the beach, all because you don't believe the sharks are there.

You might be also thinking, *"Look, you're talking about some weird spiritual battle going on, but I've got some real-life battles happening here. I need some real-life strength!"*

<u>Well, here's the kind of strength God promises</u>: Take your pick.

- Emotional Strength
- Physical Strength
- Mental Strength
- Spiritual Strength

I don't know about you, but I often catch myself praying for something like 'strength' and then forget to watch for the answer. I kind of let the distractions of the day take over. I let the ball drop in expecting and waiting to see what God's going to do. **That's a no-no.** That won't help things. So, if you catch yourself doing that, get back on track and keep reminding God of his promise and wait and watch with expectancy. Be vigilant.

Sometimes I think it's hard to muster up the faith to expect God to come through with his strength. It takes work, doesn't it? But faith isn't having the strength to go on – it's going on when you don't have the strength. It's fully expecting God to infuse you with *his* supernatural strength, even when you don't feel it yet.

Perhaps you've noticed that a lot of the promises we've covered have a lot to do with faith? In a way, it's all about living a life of faith. So, if we feel we're weak in faith, we need to fix it.

I heard it said that FAITH is - **F**ull **A**ssurance **I**n **T**he **H**eart.

QUESTION: **Are you lacking some of that assurance?**

If you're thinking, *"Well, yeah, I think I am and I don't know what to do about it?"*

The answer is kind of simple.→ Ask God to increase your faith for you. Do you think that Jesus *ignored* that man when he asked, *"I do believe, Lord, but help me overcome my unbelief."*? I don't. I think he helped the man overcome his unbelief. So, why not put it in his lap? Let him help you fix it. If you ask him to do it, he will. The key is to expect it. Don't doubt. Watch for it.

After that man asked Jesus to help him with his unbelief, his son was healed. You think that might have helped his faith? But whatever you do, just don't live in limbo. Fix it.

Wanna know a great source of strength?

Nehemiah 8:10 → *Joy* (Hebrew meaning - deep happiness and contentment), *in/of the Lord is your strength*.

You've probably heard the verse that says in God's presence is the fullness of joy (see Psalm 16:8). When you get in God's presence and stay there, you're going to have a bunch of joy. And, that joy in the Lord becomes strength to you.

Look at it this way: You can't live a life of faith without strength from God. And when God wants to make you strong, *joy* is one of the ways he does it.

Maybe you've noticed when you're discouraged or down and out, it's hard to have joy. But just as worry has no choice but to yield to faith, discouragement has no choice but to yield to joy. It can't stick around. So, use it to your advantage.

How do you get _joy_ from God?

1. We know that joy is a <u>fruit</u> of God's Spirit residing in us. When we get out of the way, and let God's Spirit lead and guide our lives, then one of the fruits that becomes evident is <u>joy</u> because we're doing what we were made to do – be led by him. (See Galatians 5:22)

2. Joy comes with <u>trusting God</u>. Romans 15:13 says that God will fill you with <u>joy</u> and peace *because* you're *trusting* him.

3. Joy comes when we have <u>hope</u>, when we truly realize the significance that we're going to be spending eternity having fun in God's kingdom. Jesus said to his followers, *"Be filled with <u>joy</u> because your names are written in heaven."* Hey, you're going to heaven...and it's going to be fun...really fun!

4. And, just like I mentioned, if you get in <u>God's presence</u> and stay there, the result will be joy in its fullest.

It's hard to have joy, though, when we're really being put through the ringer of trouble, but look at it this way → We could be wallowing in the misery of our circumstances...or... we could see it as a temporary discomfort in the light of spending *forever* free from all heartache and pain, free from anger, hatred, and evil...spending eternity having a blast learning new things, exploring the wonders of God's kingdom and his creation – the universe. It's going to be really fun...remember? **It's all a matter of our perspective, isn't it?**

Wait, sorry, I could be wrong...maybe you'd just be content to float around on a heavenly cloud and learn to play the harp and sing...forever...and ever.....and everrrrr. Just kidding.☺

Bottom-line: Don't forget that the joy that you have in God gives you <u>strength</u>. Don't live your life without it.

Every weakness I have is an opportunity for God to show me His strength. I'm thankful for my troubles...because without them, I wouldn't have experienced His strength. Anonymous

PROTECTION
<u>What God Guarantees</u>

Because God's creation has been poisoned with evil, the world has become a dangerous place. Some dangers are obvious and some are hidden. Some are from earthly origins and some are spiritual.

No matter what the dangers are, whether great or small, there are two reasons we usually seek <u>protection</u>: 1) Protection from existing *known* threats   2) Protection from potential <u>*unknown*</u> threats.

The good news is God absolutely promises his protection to his family members – that's us, against known and unknown threats, in the earthly realm as well as the spiritual realm.

But before we go over some guarantees God offers, <u>we need to clear something up</u> → **If God promises to protect us from harm, then why are so many of his children suffering** from illness, loss, troubles, and adversities?

On a more personal basis, you might be thinking → *"If God's in control and he really loves me and cares what happens to me, then <u>why is he letting this bad stuff happen to me</u>?"*

Those questions can make us wonder if God is breaking his promises, or maybe he just doesn't care.

Remember, there's evil in this world. And because there's evil, bad things happen to us. If evil weren't around there would be no suffering. None. God would be able to pour out blessings and good things into our lives without interference. But evil is present. According to Jesus, evil started with and spread from a created fallen angel, Lucifer (now called Satan). God said this about hm. *"You were blameless in your ways from the day you* *were created, until the point when <u>evil</u> was found in you."* That's when evil entered the picture. Satan became God's enemy when he chose to rebel against God. And if he's God's enemy, then he's *our* enemy too.

I know it sounds like a cop-out. – Blame it *all* on the devil. Or maybe it sounds to you like some cosmic video game – the forces of good and evil battling it out. Actually, in a way that's kind of what happened. A rebellion took place in heaven led by Lucifer (now called Satan), who was once one of God's highest angels. When God originally created millions of angels to serve in his kingdom, he didn't just want robots to carry out his will. He created them with a free-will. And, with free-will comes the possibility of disobedience and rebellion. That's exactly what happened. (If you want more details, check out the section on Trouble). Because of his judgment against Satan and the disobedient angels that followed Satan, God now has enemies that want to destroy his creation through spite and retribution. **And guess what?** If they're God's enemies, then they are now his children's enemies as well. So, troubles will come our way.

One of the enemy's favorite weapons against us is just two letters: "<u>If</u>". You can see this weapon used on Jesus when he was in the wilderness for forty days → *"<u>If</u> you are the Son of God..."* What was the enemy trying to do to Jesus? → Get him to *doubt* God. And, what's the enemy trying to do to us? → Get us to doubt God. *"<u>If</u> God really loves you, then why does he allow..."*

But the thing is, God does love us, and he wants us <u>protected</u>, so he gave us the same weapon that Jesus used against the enemy → the "<u>It is written</u>" weapon. When Jesus quoted the truth of God's Word, the enemy recoiled from him. So, that tells us something – it all comes down to the '<u>truth</u>'. We have to decide who's telling the truth? The enemy? Or God?

When the enemy whispers, *"<u>If</u> God really loves you, then why does he allow..."* Don't buy the lie. Tell the enemy the truth. Say, *"Yes, God loves me, and it is written, God says..."* Then say the scripture. It doesn't have to be those exact words. Make them your own, just as long as you believe it in your heart.

So, use the same weapon of protection Jesus used. If you choose to believe God instead of the enemy, then use *the "It is written…"* weapon. But that means you should <u>know</u> what God says in his Word and speak that truth back to the enemy (whether in your heart or out loud). → *"God says…."*

So, let's go over some promises worth claiming and speaking out about:

Psalm 121:2,7 → *I <u>realized</u> that my help and my **protection** are <u>only</u> from God, the creator of the universe. <u>He will **keep** me from</u> every danger and every form of evil as he <u>watches over my life</u>.*

Is there a greater source of help and protection that we could seek than the creator of the universe? Not that I know of.

It comes down to <u>two things</u> for that promise to work for us:
1. <u>Realizing</u> – really, truly recognizing where our help and protection are coming from in our own lives. Is it coming from sources other than God, or is God in the mix as well? Too often we leave God on the outer fringes of our lives until we really need him, and that's where he'll stay until we finally *realize* he's the *only one* who can truly protect us.

2. <u>Believing</u> -- really, truly believing God is watching over our lives and that he'll keep us from danger and all types of evil.
   So, it's <u>realizing</u> and <u>believing</u>.

And get this → The Hebrew meaning of that word "<u>*keep*</u>" in that promise, is to surround you with <u>a hedge-of-thorns</u>. Have you ever tried to get through a really thick hedge of blackberry bushes? OUCH!! It's almost impossible and it becomes hard for the enemy to get through to you as well, because God is putting a hedge of thorns around you. Wow! Just think about that for a moment. That's amazing protection. And that's what God will do for you…*if* you do your part → <u>Realize</u> and <u>Believe</u>.

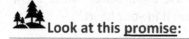**Look at this <u>promise</u>:**

Psalm 121:4,5 → *God never rests or sleeps.* <u>*God is your*</u> <u>*protector*</u>*. He* <u>*stands beside you*</u>*,* <u>*watching over you,*</u> *lovingly* <u>*protecting you*</u>*.*

That word *'<u>protector</u>"* in the Hebrew means God is your 'watchman'. It means he'll watch over you to guard and protect you and keep you safe, even when you're not aware of it. That means you can be busy with your day's activities and your watchman is right beside you, lovingly protecting you.

Do you really honestly believe that God's watching over you, that he's right beside you, to protect you? If not, then change it by making a *choice*. Make a choice to believe it. Believing always involves a choice. Something like this: *"God, your Word says you never sleep and that you lovingly watch over me to keep me safe. You promise to stand beside me, to shelter me from the storms in my life, and protect me from the effects of evil. I believe you, God, just help me with any unbelief..."*

Just remind him over and over and over again. If you're persistent, with faith mixed in, you'll see God come through on your behalf. He'll honor your faith. Why? Because <u>he always honors faith...100% of the time</u>. You're going to feel his presence beside you. You're going to see his protection in the little and big things in your life.

Just make sure you watch for it, otherwise you might miss it. I can speak from experience. There was so much God was doing for me that I missed because I thought it was just happenstance. I wasn't paying attention. I wasn't looking for it. Now I do.

By the way: Why would God need sleep? He isn't human. He doesn't get physically tired like we do. So, if you're thinking God's ignoring you or that he doesn't see what you're going through, rest assured, he's not sleeping. He notices. He says so.

Talk about being invincible. Read this guarantee:

Isaiah 54:17 God speaking → <u>*No weapons*</u> *of any form used against you will succeed...This is one of the good things my* *faithful servants* get. *Their vindication and <u>victory</u> comes from me."*

These weapons can include hurtful words and actions people use against us, ways people try to manipulate us, physical harm, and of course, the spiritual weapons of the enemy to weaken our faith, defeat us, and make us doubt God.

I hate to be a broken record here, but what will you do with this promise? <u>Don't just read it and move on</u>. Use it. Something like this → *"God, you say not one single weapon used against me will succeed. You say the victory comes from you. That means I may get attacked, but my enemies won't succeed. I may get wounded, but I'll stand strong. I receive this truth into my life because I'm your faithful servant and because you never lie..."*

Just a little reminder: Make sure you really are one of his *faithful servants*. Afterall, if we aren't faithfully obedient to God's instructions, which are meant to keep us safe from the evil-one, how can we expect to be protected against the enemy's weapons? Being a faithful servant is the *key* that makes that verse work. So, be faithful to your Father in Heaven.

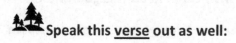**And then speak this <u>promise out</u>:**

2 Timothy 4:18 → *God will <u>rescue</u> me from <u>every</u> evil attack. In fact, he will bring me safely into his heavenly kingdom. So, all glory be to him.*

This is a great verse to declare to ourselves, to God, and to our unseen enemies in the spiritual realm, whenever we're being attacked. I like to verbally remind God of the things he promises just like the apostle Paul is doing in that verse. Somehow, by holding him to his word, it strengthens my faith. Try it with that promise. Hold God to it. Feed your faith and starve your doubt.

Speak this <u>verse</u> out as well:

✦ **Psalm 138:7** → *Even when my life is surrounded by trouble, distress, adversity, and anguish, you, God, stretch your hand out against my enemies and the power of <u>your right hand saves me</u>.*

The '<u>right hand</u>' of God, in the Old Testament, refers to God's hand of victory. When God stretches out his hand against our enemies, we can be certain we'll have the victory. We win!!!

Those last three promises we just covered involve <u>*victory*</u>, and just as that verse says, your life may be surrounded with trouble and it may be miserable to go through, but guess what? You come out the other side victorious...because God says so.

But what if you claim this promise for yourself and the trouble remains? What then? → You stand strong and wait. That's what you do. You may be surrounded by trouble on all sides, and weary from the beating you're taking, but be assured God is never late. He's always on time. He promises you victory. There's always a purpose behind his timing. It might be to test whether you really are trusting him, or maybe it's to teach you something and the trouble you're experiencing is forcing you to pay attention. Whatever the reason may be, you can be certain that God knows what he's doing and it's always to bless you in the end. Again, it may not seem like a blessing, but it is.

By the way, the context of that verse is in the 'present tense', meaning it's not a matter of *if* God will save us from troubles, but rather that he's actually in the process of doing so <u>*already*</u>. All we have to do is believe it, wait on God, and watch.

And don't forget: The <u>victory</u> may not always look like what we expected. For example, if you lost your home in a fire, God may turn around what Satan had meant for evil, by using that unfortunate circumstance to bring about a victorious outcome. Maybe it's to show others his goodness. Or maybe it's to teach others a truth. **The question is**, if God turns it into a victory, are you going to do the same?

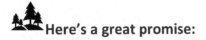 **Here's a great promise:**

✴ <u>Exodus 14:13,14</u> → *<u>Don't allow yourself</u> to be afraid in any way. <u>Keep standing strong</u>, firm, and <u>confident</u>, and <u>watch</u> God come to your rescue today. <u>God will do the fighting for you</u>. All you have to do is <u>remain calm</u>.*

I know. I underlined a bunch of words in that verse. But all of them are important. This is a <u>universal principle</u> mentioned over and over again in different ways throughout the Bible:
* Are you freaking out with worry and fear? Don't. Stay calm.
* Are you keeping strong and confident in God? If not, do it.
* Watch God come to the rescue and do the fighting for you.

Think about that → **God is doing the fighting for us. Amazing!** Yes, in this passage it was Moses talking to the Israelites, but the principles in this verse are seen all through the Bible. Moses was talking to the Israelites, who were being chased by a powerful army, the Egyptians, and now they're standing at the edge of the Red Sea, stuck, with nowhere else to go. They were cornered. **That's exactly how God likes it** – when we're cornered and there's nowhere else to turn. When we're weak, God is strong.

You know what the Israelites were doing when Moses said that statement in that verse? They were <u>complaining</u> - *"Why did God let this happen to us?"* Complaining is a *blessing-blocker*. **How about you?** What are you going to do about your situation? Complain about it...or...do what that passage says?

<u>Don't miss this</u>: In any battle, you're either in *defensive* mode or *offensive* mode. It's the same thing with the battles in your life. If you're getting pounded by the enemy just do what Jesus did when the evil-one attacked him. Go on the <u>offensive</u>.
1) He quoted scripture as a weapon. How was it a weapon? It was the truth, it was alive, and full of power. God's truth always overcomes Satan's lies. The enemy hates truth and God says there's no truth found in him. He flees from it. So, just do the same as Jesus did, keep speaking God's truth. Slice and jab!

2) He also put his circumstances into the hands of God, trusting him to fight the battle for him. He lived that verse out in his life.

Are you getting walloped by the enemy? Then, it's time to get out of *'defensive mode'* and move into *'offensive mode'*. Do your part - <u>fight back with God's Word</u>. Then, let God do his part – he'll fight the battle with you and for you. Do this and you win.

God says he will cause it to happen. That's what he guarantees:

Deuteronomy 28:7 → *God will* <u>*cause*</u> *your enemies to be defeated before you. They will attack you from one direction, but they will scatter and flee from you in seven directions.*

Why are your enemies scattering? Because God is defeating them. God's doing the scattering. The number <u>*seven*</u> in the Bible signifies 'completeness'. *Scattering* in seven directions means the complete and utter defeat of the enemy...by God.

What a great promise to hold onto. Afterall, isn't that what we want...for our enemies to flee and leave us alone?

However, that verse hinges on a <u>contingency</u>. → In the first and second verses of that same chapter in Deuteronomy 28, it says this: → *If you have* <u>*an obedient heart*</u> *and are* <u>*careful*</u> *to follow* <u>*all*</u> *of God's instructions....then the blessings of this promise will be yours.*

So, don't forget to do that. I'm sure you would agree that if we're *not* faithful to following God's instructions, then we probably aren't going to see God blessing our lives the way we hoped he would, regardless of which promise it might be.

Want the ultimate assurance? Here it is:

Romans 8:31 → *If God is for us, standing on our side, then who can stand against us and succeed* ?

The promise here is that God is on our side. He wants us to win and never lose. And, *if* he's on our side, our enemies don't stand a chance, because **God always wins**. So, speak it out. Declare it to your enemies. Feed your faith. → *"God's on my side. He's* *fighting the battle for me and God always wins. No enemy can stand against me..."*

Summary of the promises about God's protection:
What God says he will do for you:

→ God will *watch over* your life and *keep you from* every danger and every form of evil. **Trust that it's true for you. There's a hedge of thorns around you.**

→ He will stand *right beside* you to protect you. **Believe it.**

→ No *weapon* used against you (no matter what its form might be) will succeed against you. **Claim it.**

→ God will not only *protect* you from your enemies, but he'll *rescue* you from danger or take the danger away from you. **Be confident of it.**

→ God will do the *fighting for you*. Get out of the way and let him do it. **Watch for it to happen.**

→ God will cause your enemies to be *scattered* in many directions, in complete and utter defeat. **Expect it.**

→ You're *assured victory* because God will stretch out his *'right hand'* against your enemies, and whenever God does that, he always wins. So, you're victorious because God is victorious. **Live in that victory.**

Our part comes down to two things:

Look at all that God promises to do for us; then look at our responsibility. In a way, it's quite simple. Our part really comes down to two things -- *Believing* and *obeying*.

There's no room for whining that it's too hard to follow God if we just cling to these promises. God's made it super easy for us. He does all the work, and all we have to do is...*believe* and *obey*.

So, why does it seem so hard to *believe* and *obey*?

The question isn't whether we *can* or *can't* believe and obey, but whether we're *willing* to. Being *willing*, by definition, means to be ready, eager, and prepared to act. Are you willing?

The thing about faith is it doesn't require special knowledge or abilities. All of us can lay hold of faith and *decide* to live by it. As far as God's concerned, the only way to live is by faith.

Remember this verse? **2 Corinthians 5:7** → *We, as followers of God, live our lives by faith, not by how things appear to us.*

And remember that Jesus said we don't just live because we have food to eat. We live because we have his Word to feed on. But the only way his Word will benefit us is if we eat it, digest it and do it. That's what will keep us spiritually strong and healthy.

Look at the Israelites and their 40 years in the wilderness. God had promised them protection and amazing blessings if they would just *believe* in what he said he would do for them, and if they would *do* what he told them to do. But what kept them from an amazing abundant life of blessings and protection? Yup...you got it. It was their *unwillingness* to believe what God promised, and their unwillingness to do what he told them to do. They *weren't willing* to fight for and suffer if need be, to attain the promises God offered. So, what happened? They lost out on a ton of blessings. Don't let that happen to you.

It may seem foolish to some, to just blindly put our faith in the promises of God, but unless we're willing to do so, we'll never experience the blessings that are held in those promises..

Here's my question: Which would you rather do? → Doubt and receive nothing...*or*...believe and receive all that your creator offers you -- protection and an abundant life of wonderful blessings?

It all comes down to...*willingness*. And the only one who can decide that for you is...yourself.

Faith can move mountains. Doubts can create them.

Success and Prosperity
God 100% Guarantees it

It's been said: *"Money can't buy happiness, but neither can poverty."*

<u>We might as well get this straight first and foremost</u>: God does not intend for his people to live poorly. Some people think that God doesn't want them to have nice things in life. But he does. He wants his people to do well...really well. There are many promises about that in the Bible. Take this verse for example:

Psalm 35:27 → *God takes <u>great delight in the prosperity</u> of his <u>faithful servants</u>.*

You know what? That's actually a <u>guarantee</u> that God will be happy when he sees us succeeding. God, as our heavenly father, really enjoys it when his kids do well in life. It delights him. Why would he be any different from earthly parents being happy when their kids prosper and succeed in life?

It doesn't say anywhere in the Bible that God takes delight in the physical, emotional, or mental suffering of poverty in the lives of his children. He delights in their prosperity. That's what makes him happy. That's what he desires for us. It was built into his original plan for mankind way back at the beginning.

But, just as that verse says, we need to make sure we truly are his <u>servants</u> (which means doing what he tells us to do, not necessarily what we want to do). Some of God's kids don't like to think of themselves as *servants*, but (if) we want to prosper the way God wants us to, then we better <u>*be*</u> what that verse says we should be → a faithful servant.

You may already know this, but many people think that the Bible says money is the <u>root</u> of all evil. But, if they look closer, it says the '<u>*love*</u>' of money is the root of all evil. That's telling us not to love and desire money to the point that we become its *servant*...but instead, to love and desire God to the point that we become his servant (fulfilling his goodwill for our lives).

God doesn't want to hold back anything when it comes to blessing us. Check out this <u>guarantee</u>:

Romans 8:32 → *God gave us his greatest treasure as a gift. He did not even spare his own Son, but gave him as a sacrifice for us all. Since God did this for us, <u>he certainly won't hold back from any other good thing he has to give us</u>.*

Do you think that this pertains *only* to spiritual things? Nope. God's goal in sending Jesus was to restore us back to the original plan God had for humanity way back at the beginning. A large part of that <u>original plan</u> in Genesis was to bless us with good things and take good care of us on this earth. We don't have to wait until heaven, God wants to do it for us right now, right here on earth.

Let me ask you this question → What do you think God's plans are for you personally? – *Prosperity* or *Poverty*?
Read this promise. Yes...this promise again☺

<u>Jeremiah 29:11</u> God speaking→ *I know the plans I have for you. I have <u>plans to prosper you</u>, not to cause you calamity or harm; but to <u>give you</u> a future <u>filled with</u> hope and good things.*

Listen, God makes it plain as day. His plans are made crystal clear here → He plans on prospering us and giving us a future filled with hope and good things. His plans for us do not include misfortune and trouble. **Do you believe that?**

It may be weird to think of God as a planner. And it may be strange to think that <u>God *plans* on prospering us</u>. If that's what he plans for us, then is there anything that could get in *his* way? After all, God never makes mistakes, and he's never late with his timing. **But we can certainly slow him down and mess up his plans for us** by carrying out our own agenda. Have you ever done that...gotten in the way of God's good plans for you? I don't know about you, but I sometimes wonder what my life would have been like if God's plans for me were unhindered...by me.☺

You know what? People blame God for a lot of bad stuff, but one thing's crystal clear, God's blessings don't bring adversities, sickness, or poverty. Those aren't from God. That's not his heart. And he makes that clear in that promise. He specifically says his plans don't include calamity or harm. But when the enemy sends those things into our lives, God can still _use_ those situations for our good and turn them into blessings for us.

According to the Bible, God's blessings of prosperity and well-being always bring good things, without sadness attached to it. He says it right here:

✦ **Proverbs 10:22** → _It is God's blessings that bring wealth and prosperity to a person. And he adds **no** sorrow to it_.

Did you catch that? He doesn't add sorrow to his blessings. We might...but God doesn't.

If you look at all four of those verses we just covered, they are promises you can claim for yourself.

You might be thinking → _"How do I do that?"_

Answer→ By reminding God with your words. Obviously, God doesn't need reminding, but it will boost your faith when you speak it out loud. Something like this → _"God you say you enjoy it when your servants prosper. You say that if you gave us your most valued treasure - your Son, then surely you won't hold back any other blessing from me. God, you say that you have plans to prosper me, to bless me. So, as your faithful servant, I receive the good things you plan for me. You're always faithful to do what you say, so I thank you for the blessings coming my way."_
That's what you do. You remind God. Then, you watch and wait for God to act, watching with expectancy and faith mixed in.

Now, you might be thinking → *"Wait a second! Isn't that kind of selfish, to be asking for prosperity?"*

The answer is "No". Why is that? Because God is telling us in those verses what he wants to do for us. He wants to prosper us, so he expects us to expect it as well. He's always made it clear throughout the Bible that he'll pour out blessings on his *obedient* children.

All we have to do is follow what he tells us to do (*obey* his instructions), *believe* his promises, and *receive* them by faith. My, my, my...so easy...and yet...so hard to do at times.☺

Just be careful to see your blessings as God sees them. Again, if you were involved in an accident and lost your leg, God may choose to use you through that situation. Can you see it as a blessing if God turns it into one? It takes spiritual maturity to do that. But, what's the alternative...getting angry at God? Nah. If God's trying to turn your lemons into lemonade, then stop seeing your situation as a lemon, and start seeing it as lemonade. Got it?

Not to be too redundant here...but that's the key here...*faith*. After all, how can we accept the troubles in our lives if we *can't* trust God to work it all out for our good?

The question is, if life gives you a lemon, are you going to consider it a gift and trust God to make lemonade out of it?

Keep in mind, God often has *contingencies* that come with his blessings. But these contingencies are not meant to restrict us from his blessings, they're meant to protect us from missing out on all the wonderful things he wants to give us.

Just to give you an example, here's a contingency worth noting → Do you know **the first key** to opening the door to God's storehouse of blessings and prosperity? It's seeking him *first*, above all the other interests and desires we have in life.

Look at this promise:

Matthew 6:33 Jesus speaking→ *Seek God's kingdom above everything else in your life* (seek his lordship, his wisdom, his way of doing things, his realm of blessings, etc.) *and seek the right way of* *living that he prescribes. Do this and all the other things that you're striving for and are so concerned about will be added to your life* (as God sees fit).

That's the **1st key** → Seek his Kingdom *first* above anything else.

Do you see the **2nd key** that will open the door to God's prosperity and blessings? It's found in the second half of that verse above: Seeking the right way to live, as God prescribes.

God tells us in that verse he will meet every one of our needs and that it gives him great pleasure to prosper his obedient children. But, some of his children who are willing to receive his blessings still haven't seen the blessings and success, and prosperity they desire. **Why is that?**

One answer is that it takes more than just being *'willing'*. It also takes *consistently 'doing'* what God tells us to do in every area of our lives. That's what's referred to in the Bible as *'obedience'*. There are many verses in the Bible about the good things from God that will come our way *if* we would just live the way he prescribes. But many of us make it hard on ourselves by not doing that. As I've said before, God makes his way of living easy...it's just us who seem to make it hard.

There are many believers who feel they avidly obey God and still don't see the blessings we're talking about. Why is that? I personally believe that God sometimes challenges the depths of our faith. He challenges our willingness to wait on him. Are we content with where we're at, right now, as we wait? If not...why not? God wants to know if he alone is enough for us, and all the other stuff we desire we could easily leave behind. Do a heart-check. Are you content with God alone?

Bottom-line → The blessings of success and prosperity that we desire in our lives are significantly contingent on two things:
1. Seeking after God's kingdom, above everything else we're seeking in our lives.
2. Seeking the right way of living that God prescribes and then living it out in our lives.

If we do those two things, then, according to Jesus, all the other stuff we're continually striving after will be added into our lives (as God sees fit). God will <u>add</u> them to our lives, rather than us struggling so hard to *get* them. It doesn't mean we won't work hard for what we get. It just means God is the one doing the *'giving'*, even as we work for it, and we're doing the *'getting'*, offering him the honor and the glory in return.

Why did God make seeking after those two things <u>the keys</u> to prospering? Because he's all-knowing and wise and he knows material prosperity can hurt us if we aren't prepared to manage it well. If we have our priorities wrong, or we lack self-control, we can get into a heap of trouble very quickly.

So, God made sure that the <u>prosperity that comes from him</u> can only come by seeking him first, *above* everything else in our lives.

When we seek God first, we get our priorities straightened out. We gain wisdom from him on how to handle the blessings he sends us. With God being first in our lives, we'll stay away from the dangers that prosperity can entrap us in.

Money and things of prosperity deserve a proper place in our lives, but if we *don't* handle them wisely, they'll eventually rule over us with the potential to cause us problems.

And, keep this in mind → There's nothing wrong with having money and good things in your life...as long as they don't have you. Seeking God <u>first</u> and his right way of living is your safeguard from that happening.

I need to pause and make something perfectly clear here: I'm not saying that we'll *earn* God's blessings as a reward for doing good things. God doesn't measure our performance and then dole out rewards of blessings *only* if we're good.

The truth is, God is wise and his Word holds his wisdom in it. If we put into practice the things he tells us to do in his Word, it will naturally lead us to the wise management of our lives, as well as the blessings and increase he intended to give us...**guaranteed**.

Want another guarantee of prosperity and blessings in your life? Read this next verse as <u>a promise</u>:

❖ **James 1:25** → *Those who look deeply and carefully into God's Word and don't forget what it says, but instead are <u>careful to do it</u>, they will <u>prosper</u> and be <u>blessed</u> in <u>all</u> they do.*

I don't think it could get any plainer than this.→ Read (or hear) his Word and be <u>careful to do it</u>. Then you'll prosper and be blessed. It's as simple as that. It's God's guarantee to you.

🌲**Here's another guarantee for success.**

❖ **2 Chronicles 26:5** → *King Uzziah <u>continually sought God</u> during the days of the prophet Zechariah, who taught him <u>to</u> <u>fear the Lord</u>* (to live with deep respect and reverence toward God). *As long as Uzziah <u>sought guidance</u> from God, <u>followed after him</u>, and <u>obeyed</u> him, <u>God caused</u> him to <u>succeed</u>.*

Yeah, I know – lots of underlined words...again.
But there are 4 things that Uzziah did that stand out here:
1. He made sure he <u>sought</u> God consistently (not casually, but with discipline).
2. He <u>learned</u> to live with deep <u>reverence</u> toward God.
3. He <u>sought God's guidance</u> and <u>followed it</u> when it was given.
4. He <u>did</u> what God's instructions told him to do.

And, because he did all 4 of those things, God *<u>caused</u>* him to have <u>success</u>. (Hebrew meaning → God made sure that it happened).

It's no different for us. This principle is revealed all through the Bible. It's a universal truth throughout the scriptures.

God is laying out the *contingencies* for success and prosperity right there in that verse.→ If we seek after God to know him, to receive his guidance, to learn how to do what he instructs us to do, and then live them out with deep reverence toward God, he'll *<u>cause</u>* us to be blessed, and he'll help us do well in life.

Consider it to be a promise for your own success. All you have to do is follow the same steps Uzziah took and God will turn it into a guarantee. <u>Add it to your plan to do well in life.</u>

So, again, how might you declare this to God? Something like this: *"God, Uzziah was no different than me. I'm continually seeking you, and I'm heeding your guidance, and I'm living my life with deep reverence and respect toward you, carefully following your instructions. So, I'm trusting and expecting that you'll <u>cause</u> me to succeed and do well in life. For, you said it and I know it's your desire to do so. I claim this for my life, Lord."*

Put this in your gameplan to prosper and succeed in life:
1) <u>Seek</u> God consistently (not casually, but carefully)
2) <u>Live with</u> deep respect toward God (don't take this lightly)
3) <u>Follow</u> his leading (make sure you know how God leads)
4) <u>Do</u> what he says, always, not just when you feel like it

It's been said that success is a journey, not a destination.

That journey can have twists and turns and a lot of rocks and bumps to trip us up. God's Word can make the journey much smoother and safer. **Here again is that all important verse:**

<u>Psalm 119:105</u> → *Your Word God is a like a flashlight to my feet and a spotlight to my path.*

Have you ever travelled in the darkness of night on a path strewn with rocks with no light to help you along the way? I have, many times. It's tricky not to stumble. But with a flashlight, it's faster and easier. And, having a spotlight that can shine far ahead is also helpful if you want to see what direction your path is taking you. God's Word does that for you.

If you're going to succeed on the sometimes bumpy path to success, you need the guidance of God's Word to keep you from tripping or stumbling or going in the wrong direction. So, use God's flashlight. Use his spotlight. It will save you lots of trouble.

Is that verse a promise? Sort of. How could we use it? Well, instead of reminding God, we can just declare it...something like this → *"It's a promise of God that his Word will make me wise* (See Psalm 19:7). *I use it to shine a light on the paths I'm traveling on, to help me from stumbling or going astray..."*

Is your doubt keeping you from doing well in life?

You might be thinking, *"Maybe. I struggle with believing that God's promises will actually happen in my life?"*

God understands your struggles and loves you for it. He's not frowning on you. He doesn't want you to give up. He wants you to succeed in life. Keep declaring his promises throughout the day until it settles deep in your heart. Soon it will build your faith to the point where there is no doubt.

Remember:

- His promises <u>always</u> come true...even when you trust them with only a glimmer of faith.
- His Word is alive and actively working *<u>for us</u>* to build our faith.
- His Word <u>never</u> returns empty. It always accomplishes what he intended, regardless of the amount of faith we have.

Here are the 3 verses that say exactly that for us to declare.

<u>2 Samuel 22:31</u> → *"All of God's promises come true."*

<u>Hebrews 4:12</u> → *"God's word is alive and full of power, actively working for us..."*

<u>Isaiah 55:11</u> God says → *"My Word will accomplish all I want it to. It produces the results I want, everywhere I send it."*

<u>Desires</u> are what drives us in life. Having the right desires is a key to prosperity and success.

Psalm 37:4 → *Delight yourself in God and in his ways. Do this and <u>he will give you</u> the desires your heart should have.*

This is a simple promise, isn't it? If our pleasure is in God and living the way he wants, instead of just making money and increasing our possessions, then he'll change our hearts so that his desires become our desires.

Will that help us to prosper faster? Yup. Why is that? Because we won't be side-tracked with wrong desires, causing us problems and complications along the way.

Here's something we need to understand.→ **God is very wealthy**. His riches are immense. He does not act stingy toward his children. His desire is for us to have more than *just enough*.

But, even when we don't see prosperity at this point, if we delight ourselves in God, enjoying his company, his way of living, then we'll be content with where we're at in each step along the path to our successes in life.

Remember, we're not in it for the income. We're in it for the *outcome*.

🌲**Here are two promises that will also help us on the road to success and prosperity:**

You probably know this verse very well by now.

✧ **Proverbs 3:5&6** → *Put your trust in God with all your heart. Don't just rely only on your own understanding or your own judgment in each situation. Instead, in everything you do in your life, acknowledge him* (meaning - invite him into the middle of your circumstances and declare his sovereignty over your life). *Do this and he will show you which path to take, and he'll level out the obstacles that block your way.*

Here are three more things you can add to your plan for success and prosperity:

1. Put your trust totally in God's wisdom and his direction (not looking elsewhere for them)
2. Don't just rely on your own gut feeling or judgment in the situations you're in.
3. Acknowledge God, inviting him into the middle of your situations, declaring him as your King and Lord of your life.

If you do those three things, you can *expect* his guidance on your path to success and the removal of those obstacles that make your journey so much harder. That's the key – *expect* it.

Who wouldn't want the creator of the universe directing their path to success and prosperity? That's what God says he'll do. It's like having the most expensive 'success guru' as your personal business coach and wealth consultant.

And who wouldn't want their path to success to be leveled out instead of packed with hindrances and obstacles? That's part of what the Hebrew translation of the words *"He will direct your paths"* means. It certainly makes the journey much easier.

Don't forget God along the way:
After all, it's God who <u>causes</u> us to be blessed, and succeed, and to prosper. Don't take the credit for it. Stay humble. Give Him the honor. **This next verse is important**:

Deuteronomy 8:18 → *<u>Don't forget</u> it's the Lord, your God. <u>He is the one</u> that gives you the power and the ability to accumulate wealth and make you successful.*

And this verse as well:

James 1:17 → *<u>Every good thing we have</u> flows down from our Father in heaven...*

This is where having a humble heart is critical as we succeed and prosper in life. <u>Humility</u> is a big thing to God. Think about it. What led to the rebellion in heaven? It was <u>pride</u>. I think that's why God says that he hates pride and arrogance so much (See Proverbs 8:13) because it brought so much destruction to heaven and earth. **And don't miss this next promise.**

Proverbs 22:4 → *The <u>**reward**</u> for being <u>humble</u> and <u>deeply respecting God</u> in your life will be **wealth, prosperity, honor, and an abundantly flowing life**.*

<u>Wealth</u>, <u>prosperity</u>, <u>honor</u>, and an <u>abundant life</u>. Wow!!! Who wouldn't want all that? If God goes out of his way to reward <u>humility</u> and <u>respect toward him</u> with those amazing rewards, then being humble and respectful to God must be pretty important to him, don't you think?
So, you might want to add these two things to your plan for success and prosperity:

1. Be <u>humble</u> → The Hebrew meaning of the word *'humble'* is having an honest view of yourself, not thinking you're more important than others. It's giving more honor, value, and importance to God and other people than you do yourself. Pride is centered on *'self'* – It's all about *'whats in it for me'* It's a *blessing-blocker*, so stay humble.

2. Live with <u>deep reverence and respect for God</u>. That word in the Hebrew means to use serious caution and self-evaluation to avoid anything that would offend or grieve God.

   What's the <u>result</u> if we do these two things? → <u>Wealth</u>, <u>prosperity</u>, <u>honor</u>, and an <u>abundant life</u>. – Nice, huh? ☺

Ok, here are a few promises that require us to do something that doesn't come naturally. But the blessings of success and prosperity are absolutely huge:

Read this promise → I call it **The Recipe For Success**. God spoke it to Joshua, but it's a universal principle that God teaches throughout the scriptures. So, it's meant for us as well.

<u>Joshua 1:7,8</u> → Be *<u>careful</u>* to *<u>obey</u>* *<u>all</u>* the instructions God gives you in his Book. *<u>Don't waver</u>* nor *<u>deviate</u>* from them, not even a small amount. *<u>If you do these things</u>*, **then** you'll gain insight and *you'll* **prosper** and **succeed** in everything you do.
Also, *<u>study</u>* God's Book of Instructions. *<u>Ponder and think about it</u>* often throughout your days and nights, *<u>**so that** you will be sure to</u>* do everything written in it. **Only then**, will you prosper, do well in life, and succeed in all you do.

Yeah, I know. I underlined a bunch of words...again. Sorry, but I need you to take note of them...they're important.

Again, here are <u>two more things</u> we can add to our plan for prosperity and success in this life.
Twice in this passage, God says that we'll prosper, and succeed, and do well in life *(if)* we:

1. Simply <u>do</u> what God tells us to do, <u>without *wavering*</u> or *straying*.

2. <u>Study</u> his Book of Instructions, and <u>meditate on it</u> in order to understand it, <u>so that</u> we'll be sure to do it.

By the way, do you know what <u>*wavering*</u> is? It's riding the fence of obedience and disobedience. It's never really taking a stand on one side or the other. Sometimes we'll do what God says and sometimes we'll do our own thing. There's no consistency. Back and forth. That's *wavering*.

So, here's the thing: If you want God's guarantee of prosperity and success to become a reality in your life then you can't waver from God's instructions. Remember his instructions help you and protect you. So no wavering or deviating allowed. God says it's an all-or-nothing deal. He'll do his part (*if*) we do ours.

Do you know what the word '<u>study</u>' means in that verse? It means we're not just opening God's Word and randomly picking some passage to read. Nope, that won't work here. Instead, we have to <u>know</u> and <u>understand</u> what the passage means, and then we <u>chew on it over and over</u> in our minds and hearts <u>so that we'll be sure</u> to apply them to our lives. That's the key here. We're not just reading his instructions and closing the book. No, <u>we're *doing* them</u>. And as that promise says: ***Only then***, will you prosper, do well in life, and succeed in all you do.

That's what's going to lead to blessings and increase in our lives. <u>Here's an example</u>: If we go to a doctor with a significant health issue, we don't want him to have only read about the different tests he could do. Right? We want him to have experience...to know what the tests are, how to do the tests, understand what they mean, and how to apply them to our body so we'll get good results. It's the same with God's Word.

KUA = <u>K</u>now it, <u>U</u>nderstand it, <u>A</u>pply it to your life.

What happens if we *don't* study and meditate on God's instructions as that passage instructs us to do? What if we just casually read his Word? Chances are we'll forget it and start to waver and deviate from it. God doesn't want that to happen to us. He wants us to win in life, so he gave us that passage to lead us to success, prosperity, and blessings.

All we have to do is follow God's <u>Recipe For Success</u>.

🌲 **Want another recipe for prosperity and success?**

✦ <u>**Psalm 1:1-3**</u> → *A person <u>will be blessed</u> **if** they don't live their life according to the advice of people who rebel against God. They'll <u>experience blessings</u> **if** they don't hang around people who continually choose to do what's wrong instead of what's right.*
<u>Instead</u>, that person finds pleasure in following God's instructions, thinking about them often throughout their days and nights. That person will be well watered, just like a tree that's been planted by a stream of water; it will produce beautiful fruit in its season and its leaves will not wither. In fact, <u>everything that person does will succeed and prosper</u>.

If you want to prosper and succeed and be blessed, then add these 3 things to your plan to do well in life.
1.   Watch out <u>where you get your advice from</u>, especially from people that aren't interested in following God.
2.   Watch out <u>who you hang out with</u>, especially people that choose to live wrongly before God.
3.   <u>Find pleasure in *doing* God's Word</u> and make an effort to think about it throughout the day, so you'll be sure to do it.

What will these 3 things do for you? → They'll cause you to be a wise and fruitful person in life (like that tree); **plus,** you'll make progress in your endeavors, prospering and succeeding at *whatever* you do. That's what that promise guarantees us.

By the way, the Hebrew word in that verse for '*<u>prosper</u>*' doesn't necessarily mean getting rich. It means to do well and to advance in life, to bring success, happiness, and prosperity into your life — personally, materialistically, and spiritually. Is that what you want? Go and get it. God wants you to have it.

🌲***Look at this next guarantee:*** God made this promise to Joshua, but it also applies to us as well because it's universally expressed to all of God's people throughout the Bible. So, receive it for yourself!

✢ **1 Chronicle 22:13** → *You will* <u>*prosper*</u> *and be* <u>*successful*</u> ***if*** *you are* <u>*careful*</u> *to obey* <u>*all*</u> *that God tells you to do in his instructions.*

And look at this promise as well:

✢ **1 King 2:3** → *Walk through life in* <u>*obedience to God*</u>*, and* ***keep*** <u>***all of his instructions***</u> *that are written in his Book of Instructions.* <u>*Do this,*</u> ***so that*** *you may* <u>*prosper and succeed*</u> *in* <u>*all*</u> *you do and wherever you go.*

There it is again (the "O" word) – *obedience* – doing what God tells us to do. There are many verses in the scriptures that say the same thing. **It seems pretty simple, doesn't it?** If we want to do well in life and enjoy prosperity and success, then just do what he tells us to do. It's for our own wellbeing anyway.
So, why do so many of us struggle with it?
I personally believe it comes down to who's sitting on the throne in our lives. <u>Who's in charge?</u> God or us? If it's God, then all of his instructions become a lot easier to follow, and blessings and prosperity will follow. If it's us, then things get a whole lot harder.

If we want God to prosper us, and if we want him to help us succeed, then we need to **MAC** it. (Make **A** Choice) → Who's going to be on the throne?

Just a Sidenote: That phrase "***keep*** <u>***all of his instructions***</u>" in that second verse above; in Hebrew it means to guard and put a hedge of thorns around his instructions. That's what God wants us to do with his Word...not just <u>read</u> it and <u>do</u> it, but ***guard*** <u>**it**</u> with a hedge of protection from an invasion from the enemy.

People who don't know God's Word have holes in their hedges and the enemy can sneak right in and cause havoc. Don't let that happen to you. Not *guarding* God's Word can cause holes in the hedge. That's a *blessing-blocker*. Guarding his Word leads to prosperity and success. Knowing this principle is important.

Guarding his Word means God's Word is a necessity for us, as though we can't live without it and nothing's going to keep us from it. Dare I say that we should even *love* his Word...for the truth it gives, the wisdom it provides, and the life it breaths into our soul. God never intended the life of a believer to be just lived by a set of rules. He wants us to have a heart for his Word. Too many believers live their lives by the letter of the law, not because they want to do it, but because they're *supposed* to do it. But God wants us to have a heart-felt desire to know what he says and what he thinks. Do you have that desire? It will only develop within us when we spend time with him and guard his Word as though we can't live without it.

Zig Ziglar once said: *"Money can't make you happy...but everybody wants to find out for themselves."* ☺

If that's you, then here are a few warnings, and if you heed them, they'll save you a lot of time and discouragement in your path to finding God's blessings and prosperity. *Check this out:*

Luke 16:11 Jesus speaking→ *If you've not been shown to be trustworthy with your worldly wealth and possessions, then how can you be trusted with the true riches of heaven?*

God wants to trust us with his true riches which will always bless other people, as well as ourselves. But he knows he can't do that if we're not faithful with what he's already given us in our lives, our jobs, and our businesses.

Matthew 6:19 Jesus speaking→ *Don't just accumulate for yourselves riches and possessions in your earthly life, where they can break down, be lost, or stolen. Instead, accumulate riches for yourself in heaven where they will last forever and never lose their value.*

What are the true riches of God? They are riches that will last for eternity – like wisdom, true understanding, happiness, joy, peace, patience, love, kindness, and the list goes on. And God wants to entrust those spiritual riches into our lives, knowing that we'll handle them with care. **All of them come from the**

wealth and possessions of God. They are what the Bible calls *"gold and silver"*, compared to all of the temporal earthly riches and accomplishments that it calls *"wood, hay, and dust"*.

And look at this verse:

✦ **1 Corinthians 3:12,13,15** → *When we stand before God, fire will reveal the value of the actions and motives of our lives – gold and silver, or wood, hay, and dust. And if our deeds survive, we'll be <u>blessed and rewarded</u> by God. But if our deeds are burned up, we'll suffer a <u>great loss</u>.*

Which do you think will last through eternity? The gold and silver, or the wood, hay, and dust? Which do you think will come through the fire of God's assessment of our lives when we finally stand before Him? That's right, the gold and silver. The wood, hay, and dust will be burned up. <u>It doesn't have eternal value</u>. It's worthless in the light of eternity and what God values in us. It won't hold up to the fire of God's assessment. So, we need to make sure we're faithful to God in all our endeavors, whether work or play, from the big things all the way down to the little things...chasing after what's important to God – the eternal gold and silver, not the temporary wood, hay, and dust. If we don't...we'll suffer <u>a great loss</u>. → Ponder that thought.

It was a turning point in my life when I realized that most of the things I'd done in life and most of my accomplishments on this earth were nothing but wood, hay, and dust. I was striving for the *'good life'* until I realized most of it wouldn't last; that it would easily be burned away by the fire of God's assessment of my life. It scared me to think there would be nothing of eternal value to show for my life when I stood before him. It caused me to change my priorities and invest in the eternal gold and silver— the stuff that truly matters, the stuff that lasts forever.

✦ **Luke 12:34** Jesus speaking→ *Where your true treasure is in your life, that's where the desires of your heart will be also.*

So, what do we do with those last three verses? I suggest **MAC**'ing it.→ **M**ake **A C**hoice early on, that from now on we'll make it a priority to focus our hearts on storing up heavenly wealth first and foremost – the true treasures of heavenly gold and silver. After all, if we truly understand what the last three verses are saying, then it leaves only two choices.→ Either live for God or live for ourselves.

So, put this in your plan for prosperity and success in this life: Live for the true heavenly gold and silver. Stay away from the wood, hay, and dust.

Art Buchwald once wrote, *"The best things in life aren't things."* How true! That's what we're talking about here, right?

Ponder this next verse:

 Matthew 16:2 Jesus speaking→ *What does it benefit you if you gain all the wealth and possessions this world has to offer, but you forfeit your life in the process? After all, what is more, valuable than the eternal worth of your soul?*

You already know this, but it's worth repeating. → Our lives are shaped by the choices we make, and ultimately, it's our responsibility to make the choices we're willing to live with...for eternity.

Don't build your success alone:

Psalm 127:1 → *Unless God is involved in building the house, the workers' labor is in vain.*

Notice it's <u>both</u> the workers and God that are supposed to be building the house. **There is a physical aspect and a spiritual aspect to what we do in life.** If we don't have *both* involved, we could risk being misguided and miss the blessings God wanted to give us. It could be a *blessing-blocker*. So, <u>let God be involved in building your success</u>. Invite him to be right there in the middle of it all. If he's not...well then...good luck.☺

Many believers think seeking after success is wrong...that it's selfish. But that's contrary to what God says. All through the Bible God tells us he wants us to seek success. In fact, he tells us *how* to do it, and then he *helps* us to do it. God wants to help *build* your success, otherwise you're doing it alone. He wants to be right there in the middle of it all. So, don't forget to make him your foreman. Remember...he holds the blueprints.

And here's the final thing we need to cover: Don't miss this. It's important:

2 Corinthians 9:8 → *God is happy to give you <u>more than you need</u>, so you'll have plenty of everything you need and <u>enough left over to share with others</u>.*

That's amazing when you think about it. **God wants to give us more than what we need**. Why is that? So, we'll share it with others. But you know what we end up doing? Keeping it all for ourselves. Don't do that. That's a *'blessing-blocker'*. I think it was the Red Hot Chili Peppers that sang, *"Give-it-away, Give-it-away, Give-it-away, now."* Yeah, I know, that song's ancient, but that's what we're talking about, right? And hey...don't give it *alllll* away. Keep some of it for yourself.☺

How is this a promise you can claim? → *"God, you say that you're happy to give me <u>more than I need</u>, with enough left over so I can share with others. I would love to see you do that. I'm receiving this promise from you and I'll live up to my end of the blessing. I'll be generous and share with others."*

Anne Frank once wrote: *"No one has ever become poor by giving."* There's a lot of truth to that statement, isn't there?

Whatever wealth and possessions we've accumulated in life, they're ultimately given to us by God. They're ultimately his anyway, if he's the king of our lives. Right? So, <u>nothing we have should be held onto too tightly by us</u>. Be generous and share it with others. What do you have to lose, but the extra stuff God gave you in the first place. And don't give junk. Give the best.

Winston Churchill once said: *"We make a living by what we get, but we make a life by what we give."*

Here's an amazing guarantee:

Luke 6:38 Jesus speaking → *Give to others <u>generously</u> and it will be given back to you <u>generously</u>. You will be given <u>so much more in return</u>, that it will be poured out into your life with* *no space left for more. For, the amount you give to others will determine the measure you will receive in return.*

That's a wonderful promise. Give generously and get much, much more in return. Those returns sound better than the stock market, don't they?

Just don't miss the last part of that verse. The amount you give to others will determine how much you'll receive in return. That can be exciting to hear…or…it can be a bit unsettling. If we're *not* giving generously, we're *not* going to be getting generously. There's no way around it. Want to get a lot? Then give a lot. Hey, Jesus said it, not me! So, give and get. Be a wise investor. Invest in heavenly gold and silver…and be generous in giving your life away. Not doing so is a *blessing-blocker*. You don't want that do you?

Let's put all of these promises and guarantees together:

Here's what you need to do to become a wise and fruitful person in life, whose success and prosperity are a testimony of God's goodness in your life.

12 things to add to your plan to succeed and do well in life:

1. Get comfortable with the idea that God is happy to prosper you and give you success in life.
2. Seek God's kingdom above everything else in your life, and all the other stuff you're striving for will be provided by God himself, as he sees fit.
3. Seek to consistently live your life the way God prescribes.
4. Take pleasure in being in God's company and he will align your desires with his.
5. Look into God's Word carefully. Ponder it frequently, and then do what it says. No wavering or deviating allowed.
6. Use God's Word as a flashlight to keep you from stumbling and use it as a spotlight to see which direction to take.

7. Put your trust in God's wisdom and direction. Don't just trust your own judgment. Acknowledge God and invite him into the middle of each situation so he can direct your paths.

8. Don't forget that it's God who *causes* you to prosper, succeed and do well in life.

9. Be humble about your blessings, prosperity, and success.

10. Be careful to live your life with deep respect and reverence toward God.

11. Be generous and share with others the blessings God's given you.

12. Store up for yourself heavenly treasures. Make sure it's gold and silver and *not* wood, hay, or dust.

Do these things and God <u>guarantees</u> that you will prosper, do well, and succeed in life.

<u>And Remember:</u>
God's idea of true success is when it ends up making a difference in the lives of others, not just our own.

Joy
What God Guarantees

With the world as crazy as it is, we all need a dose of joy, don't we? Joy is extremely important to us believers. Why? Because you need to have it if you're going to live as an *overcomer* in this world. The joy of/in the Lord is our strength, and you need strength if you're going to *win* the battles in your life.

But what exactly is joy (can you define it?) and how do we get it and keep it?

What is joy? → It isn't necessarily happiness. You can be unhappy in the most miserable of circumstances and still have *joy*. So, joy doesn't depend on whether things are going well for us or not.

Worldly joy can be fickle. It comes and goes depending on our circumstances. **Spiritual joy**, however, can last regardless of our circumstances. In other words, bad stuff that happens to us can't take away the joy God gives us…. unless we let it.

Joy can be described as a calm inner gladness and contentment. I like that…short but sweet.

But here's the thing about joy…it involves a choice.
Do you remember this next verse? We covered it in the section on Trouble?

James 1:2 → *When you run into a lot of problems, or encounter a bunch of trials or adversities, consider it a joy and be glad it's happening.*

WHAT??? Yup…think of it as an opportunity to have joy. How's that possible? The answer is in **verse 3** →

✦ **Verse 3** → *Because those trials are going to challenge and grow your faith. And when you make it through all that trouble, still holding tightly to your faith, you'll be even stronger when more trials come down the road.*

Yikes!!! That doesn't sound very fun to me. How 'bout you? Nevertheless, did you notice the two words –"*consider it*"? That's the choice that we have to make. How are we going to *consider* the situation we're in? Are we going to look at our crummy circumstances we're going through as a chance to have joy and grow from them...*or*...are we going to complain and be inwardly angry at God for letting that stuff happen to us?

Here's that 3 letter idiom...again → MAC it.→ **M**ake **A** **C**hoice
When we make a choice and not wallow in the indecisiveness of how we're going to consider our trials, it can change our lives in dramatic ways. Something happens within our mindset and our attitude. We become stronger in our trust and faith.

🌲**C.S. Lewis once wrote:** *"Joy is the serious business of heaven."* I like that quote because, in the next verse, Jesus is serious enough about his words that he goes out of his way to make sure we know that the things he's telling us will help us have joy and keep it flowing in our lives.

✦ **John 15:8-11** Jesus speaking → *My father in heaven is glorified and honored when you produce much fruit. I have loved you just as my father in heaven has loved me. So, remain in my love.* (Here's how) *When you obey my instructions, you remain in my love, just as I obey my father's instructions and thus remain in his love.*
I have told you these things so that my joy will be in you and that your joy may be full.

Go backward in this passage.→ Notice two joys are mentioned here. One is Jesus' joy and the other is our own joy. Why are there two joys mentioned?
One answer is that we need lots of things that come from God himself in order to survive this life – things like his joy, his

peace, his strength, his hope, his wisdom, his love etc. Without his traits operating in us, it's practically impossible to live the life God wants for us all on our own.

There are <u>two other things</u> in that verse that are worth mentioning *if* we want to have joy and be able to keep it. Did you catch them?
1. Producing a lot of fruit.
2. Remaining in his love.

In that verse, Jesus said he told us those two things **'so that'** we would have *his joy* <u>in us</u> and *our own joy* would be <u>full</u>?
The two words '<u>so that</u> are important here. Why? Because we need to produce much fruit *and* remain in his love <u>so that</u> we'll have <u>joy</u>. **In other words**, we're not going to have joy unless we have those two aspects present in our walk with God.

Well, how do we get joy from being fruitful or remaining in His love?
1.) Look at it this way: Whenever we're really productive and fruitful at work or at home, it gives us a sense of satisfaction and joy. Right? It's the same way in God's kingdom.→ When we're producing spiritual fruit (not just some fruit...but *"much fruit"*) in our walk with God, it's going to give us that same result – satisfaction and joy.

2.) Combine that with *'remaining in his love'* (meaning, being in the center of his love, spending time with him, letting him teach us), well, you can imagine that we're going to have a lot of joy if we do all that. Because, when you think about it when we're right dab in the middle of almighty God's love, it's all good. It brings *joy*.

So, <u>producing a lot of fruit</u> and <u>remaining in his love</u> will bring us joy.

We've covered this next promise before, but it's worth mentioning it again.

<u>Jeremiah 29:11</u> God speaking → *I am certain of the <u>plans</u> I have for you, to give you <u>great peace</u> and well-being, to <u>prosper</u>*

you, not to cause you trouble. I want to give you <u>a future that's</u>
<u>*filled with hope*</u>.

God has plans to *personally* give us great peace, well-being, prosperity, and a future filled with hope. Wow! Who wouldn't want that? If we really believe that, shouldn't it bring <u>joy</u> to our hearts? I mean, it's not just spiritual 'fluff'. God guarantees it. Shouldn't we *expect* it to happen in our lives here on earth?

And since we're talking about God's good intentions for us, read this promise. It should also give us joy:

<u>**James 1:17**</u> → <u>*Every*</u> *good gift* (Greek meaning - pleasant things that make us happy and give us joy) *comes down to us from God, our father in heaven.*

God's the giver of good things and he's looking for people he can give them to – that's us! What's the point of having good things to give if there's no one on the receiving end. So, if you have good things in your life, chalk it up to God. And if you have bad things in your life...*don't* chalk it up to God. That's the enemy's fault. God may *allow* it for various reasons, but he knows what's going on, and he cares about you. He can turn the bad into good, even if we don't see it at the time.

In that previous verse about God's plans for us, did you notice that part of his plans is <u>*not*</u> to cause us trouble (evil)? The meaning in Hebrew is that God has <u>no plans</u> to cause us pain, unhappiness, misery, sadness, distress, injury, wrong or evil.

Remember what Jesus said about who causes that stuff? It's the thief (the evil-one) that comes to steal from us those good things from God, to destroy our lives any way he can, and even kill us (See John 10:10). Then, Jesus added that he, himself, came to us so that we could have <u>an abundant life</u>.

It's not God that makes bad things happen in our lives. It's usually the evil-one, the enemy of our souls who wants to steal our *joy* from us. God may allow trouble to come for good and godly reasons, but he usually doesn't cause it...he *allows* it. He's the giver of <u>*every*</u> good thing that brings joy. Rememberize it☺

Want a **guarantee** of joy in your life?

Psalm 16:11 → *In His presence is the* <u>*fullness of joy*</u>.

It doesn't say *"In His presence you may or may not have joy."* No, it's saying that if we hang out <u>in God's presence,</u> we are <u>guaranteed joy</u>...and not just *some* of it – it says we'll be filled <u>to the brim</u> with it. That's what the Hebrew word for *'*<u>*fullness*</u>*'* means in that verse – to be filled to the <u>brim</u>...with joy.
And you know what? → When we're in God's presence, and joy is filling us to the brim, there's <u>no room left for</u> sadness, despair, hopelessness, or depression. That's amazing, isn't it?

 Look at these 3 verses:
Psalm 95:1&3 → *Sing with* <u>*joy*</u> *to the Lord.*
Psalm 84:2 → *My heart sings with* <u>*joy*</u> *to the living God.*
Psalm 100:2 → *Enter God's presence with* <u>*joyful*</u> *singing.*

You know what these verses have in common? Yup. Singing.
I don't know about you, but what those verses are talking about doesn't come easy for me. All I can say is, in God's presence there's a lot of joy and it probably leads to a lot of singing. So, it's probably good for us to express that feeling back to God. In other words, joy seems to be a 2-way process. → God promises us joy as we immerse ourselves in his presence, and then we express it back to him in some form...like singing. I hope He has earplugs if he hears me howling away. I'm serious!!!.☺

Here's an important verse:

Jeremiah 15:16 → *I listened to your* <u>*words*</u> *carefully and they* <u>*brought joy*</u> *to my heart and made me very happy because I've been called by your name.*

It's not just being in his presence that promises us joy....it's also being in God's Word. I don't know if you experience this, but reading God's Word brings a lot of people joy.

If you struggle with enjoying his Word, don't feel bad. That was me at one time. It could be a couple of things:

1.) Some <u>Bible translations</u>, like the King James Version, are super-hard for many people to grasp. I have nine years of university education and I scratch my head when I read it. I mean think about it. It's written in a language a few hundred years old. We don't even talk like that anymore, so it's hard to read. Pick a translation that speaks to your heart. That's where God speaks to us...on the heart-level.

2.) Speaking of heart-level, <u>do a heart-check</u>. If you're truly honest with yourself, maybe there's something missing in your walk with God that's keeping you from enjoying reading his Word or spending time with him. Whatever you do, don't beat yourself up. God totally understands you. He's in love with you and wants you to win at life. You're his very own child. So, whatever's missing, make it right, and get on with the *joy*.

Want God to straight-out *give* you joy? *Then read this next guarantee:*

<u>Ecclesiastes 2:26</u> → *When people please God by doing what he tells them to do, <u>he will give them</u> wisdom, understanding, and <u>joy</u>.*

That's a good promise to grab onto. Do what God tells you to do (consistently) and he'll give you wisdom on how to live your life, along with an understanding of the things of God. And he'll give you <u>joy</u>, just like that verse says. Why would we have joy from doing those things? Because, inwardly, we know we are doing what pleases God. That's how we were made...to please God and he us. We weren't made for doing what's wrong. No one ever has true joy from doing what is wrong.

Here's another guarantee worth grabbing:

<u>Psalm 19: 7&8</u> → *God's instructions can be trusted. They make <u>foolish</u> people <u>wise</u>. God's instructions are the right thing for your life and doing them <u>bring joy to the heart</u>.*

Do you see it? You can trust God's instructions as the right way to live. Doing God's way of living brings joy to the inward part of us. Doing what's wrong doesn't.

You know what that verse is also saying? → If you've made foolish mistakes in your life, you don't have to anymore. Just follow God's instructions and you'll <u>gain</u> wisdom. And *if* you <u>apply</u> that wisdom to your life, then chances are you'll be making far fewer mistakes...and that should make you happier. It will bring joy to your heart.

Kind of weird, isn't it? It seems God makes it so simple to have peace and joy...but somehow...we make it hard.

We make it hard on ourselves when we allow joy to be stolen from us → The only thing that can really steal our joy from us...is <u>sin</u>. That's right...the "S" word.☺ I'll tell you something, I don't feel very happy or joyful when I've done what I know is wrong in God's eyes. How about you?

It's been said: *"Forbidden fruit creates many jams."* So, stop messing with the blessing! Don't eat the bad fruit. ☺

Check this promise out:

<u>Ephesians 1:3</u> → *God has blessed us with each and <u>every</u> <u>spiritual blessing that comes **from him**</u>, from his heavenly realm, all because we're united with Christ Jesus.*

What kind of spiritual blessings is he talking about?

*<u>His Supernatural **Strength**</u> – <u>**Philippians 4:13**</u>→ "I can handle anything life throws at me, by relying on Christ who gives me <u>his</u> supernatural strength."*

*<u>His Supernatural **Peace**</u> – 2 <u>**Thessalonians 3:16**</u>→ The Lord of Peace himself will give you <u>his</u> supernatural peace at <u>all</u> times and in <u>every</u> situation.*

*<u>His Supernatural **Hope**</u> – <u>**Romans 15:13**</u>→ May, God, the <u>source</u> of hope fill you with <u>his</u> joy and peace, all because you fully trust him. Then, through the power of the Holy Spirit <u>you will overflow with hope</u>.*

You get the idea...God gives us <u>his own personal supernatural stuff</u> so we can thrive on this earth, not just survive.

What do those things have to do with <u>joy</u>? → Well, if we walk around each day filled with God's own stuff inside us (like His strength, His peace, His hope, etc.) we're most likely going to have a lot of <u>joy</u> as a result, wouldn't you agree?

Lastly, here's a healthy promise. It's in Proverbs.

Wait! Can a proverb be a promise? Yup. Here's why → The book of Proverbs holds the wisdom of God, and God's wisdom is truth, and truth means it will always come true. That's what makes a proverb a promise...it will always come true.

So, here's the <u>guarantee</u>:

<u>Proverbs 17:22</u> → *A heart that has <u>joy</u>, brings health and healing to the body and soul.*

We've already seen that God's <u>peace</u> brings a good night's rest and health to the body. Now we see <u>joy</u> does the same thing – health and healing to the mind and body. Medical science has numerous studies on the health benefits of joy and peace. Google it. God already knew it. He was way ahead of Google and medicine, and that's why he guarantees it to his kids.

So, what do you think we need a daily dose of? Yup. <u>Joy</u> and <u>peace</u>. You know what I say? → If the Great Physician is prescribing his *joy* and his *peace* to us, then may he give us a double dose!

> **The more the heart is sated with joy,**
> **the more it becomes insatiable.**
> Gabrielle Roy

Guidance
What God Promises

If you can tell the difference between good advice and bad advice, you don't need advice. - Laurence Peters

Do you know what I think is the hardest challenge for any follower of God? → It's learning how to hear from Him.

Let's say that you were offered a job in a different area of the country. It's a great job offer, with better pay, and the weather's ideal. Should you take it or not? You could go to God's written Word and receive general advice and guidance, but it won't tell you whether to take the job or not. Right?

The good news is that God loves to talk to us. We just need to learn to listen to his voice.

God's already figured it all out for you.

Jeremiah 29:11 God speaking→ *I know my plans I have for you. They are plans to help you prosper...*

The first thing we need to realize is God's got it all figured out. He *already* has plans for us. And you know what that does? It takes all the pressure off us and puts it on God. They may not be our plans, but rest assured, his plans are always good plans, to help us do well in life. That's what he says in that promise. He's *already* figured out our future. All we need to do is <u>cooperate</u> with him so he can bring it about.

But you know what can be a *blessing-blocker*? → When we mess up God's plans for us – when we get *in the way* instead of being *part of the way*. That will only happen when we don't let him lead.

That's what happened to the Israelites when they left Egypt. God didn't expect them to make their way alone through the desert without his help. He wanted to guide them. But they didn't trust him. When things got hard, they messed up God's plans for them because they focused on the hardships and refused to cooperate along the way to the Promise Land. Did they lose out? Oh yeah! They could have had a great journey had they just trusted God as they went. You know what? It's the same with us. Trust or no trust, that's essentially the question.

Do you know what we tend to do? → When we have a problem we're encountering, or a decision we need to make, and we don't know which direction to go, we often focus only on the problem itself. We dwell on it, and fret about it, and seek advice from friends and family. **But that's not where our focus should be, right?** It should be on letting God guide us, by seeking his Word and listening to his Spirit who lives inside us. That's where we'll find reliable guidance that's always correct for us. We can never go wrong with it. I'm not saying don't talk with friends and family about it. They may have just the right advice you need. I'm just saying make God the main source of your counsel and guidance. He should have the final say...always.

And don't forget this: God's Word says the Holy Spirit is our Counselor, meaning he'll advise us on the details of our lives. So, why not use his counselling service. Afterall. it's FREE! ☺

The challenge for many of us might be that we don't know how to hear from the Holy Spirit, or maybe we don't give him our attention. Many of us may not have been taught much about him. But, an easy way to listen to the Holy Spirit is to just talk with him. He's real. He's not some cosmic entity who sits in the background of our lives. He was sent to live in us by God so he can guide us and help us along the way. So, he should be front and center in our lives. Jesus told us that he was not leaving us alone when he returned to heaven. He said he was sending the Holy Spirit to be *with* us *and* in us, to be our Comforter, our Encourager, our Helper, and our Counselor. (See John 14 16&17)

Check out these 3 verses (There are more, but we'll stick with these)

✦ **John 14:16** Jesus speaking → *I will ask my Father in heaven to give you another <u>counselor</u>* (Greek meaning – advisor, comfortor, encourager, strengthener, helper, one who will assist you). *He will act as <u>my representative</u>, and he will always be with you. He will <u>lead you</u> into all truth...*

✦ **John 16:13** Jesus speaking → *When I send the Holy Spirit to you, <u>he will guide you</u> and help you understand the truth. He won't be speaking on his own, but <u>he will only tell you what he has heard from me</u>.*

✦ **1 Corinthians 6:19** → *Understand this, you are the temple of the Holy Spirit <u>who lives in you</u> and <u>was given to you by God</u>.*

What do those verses tell us? That God sent the Holy Spirit to us, and placed him inside us, to personally guide us, advise us, and help us. That way we would have God with us always. He did it so we would be assured of success in our dealings in life. But I think many of us don't avail ourselves of his help. How much more would we be sure of our decsisions in life if we let God's Spirit counsel and guide us.

Here's the Bottom-line→ Want some advice? Want some comfort and encouragement? Need some strength, or some help? Then ask the Holy Spirit for it. That's why he's there alongside you, to give you those things. Don't ignore him.

I can promise you this: If you talk to the Holy Spirit, you will receive an answer. And, just as that 2nd verse says, because he tells us only what he hears from Jesus, <u>we can trust it to be the best advice and guidance we can receive</u>. He'll nudge you, and whisper to you, and point things out. If you pay attention to him, you'll receive the guidance you're seeking. **So, you want some guidance from God?** → Talk to the Holy Spirit.

🌲*Need some light on your situation? Some wisdom? Some insight toward a solution? Check this promise out:*

✦ **Psalm 119:130** → *God's Word gives _light_ so that even those who lack direction and understanding are given _insight_ and are made wise.*

And this promise:

✦ **Psalm 119:105** → *Your Word, God, is a flashlight for my feet* (to keep me from stumbling) *and a spotlight to my path* (so I can see where I'm heading).

There are 3 things God promises us in these two verses:

1. If we use his Word for guidance, we'll be <u>given insight</u> that will <u>help us act wisely</u> and keep us going the right direction.
2. Applying his Word to our lives will <u>keep our feet from stumbling</u> so we won't make mistakes and get into trouble.
3. His Word will <u>show us the right path</u> to travel on so there's no confusion, no wondering. We won't be in the dark.

Think about this→ Have you ever been in a room that's dark, and you tried to make your way around, only to stumble and bump into things? That's kind of what it's like when we don't have God's guidance in our lives. **What's interesting to me** is that a single little match can light up an entire room. Do you think it's a coincidence that light always dispels darkness, but darkness can never dispel light? I think it's a spiritual principle that God made unchangeable. God's Word is light and it dispels the darkness in our lives. It helps us see clearly and that's what we want, isn't it?

So, you know what I say? Don't waste time trying to stumble your way through your circumstances. Use God's guidance as you travel through life. <u>Use the light of his Word</u> to find your way. It'll drive out that darkness, save you time, and keep you from missteps.

Always remember that the more you're familiar with God's voice in his Word, the easier it will be to recognize his voice in your heart, for it will always agree with his Word.

How could you personally use those two promises we just covered to help guide your way? I would recommend speaking them out to God. **Maybe something like this→** *"God, you say your Word will give me insight and wisdom...which is what I need right now. As I use your Word for my light, I receive the insight and wisdom you give through it. I expect your Word to shine its light on the path I'm on, to guide my decisions..."*

Here are three promises that are encouraging if you want God to guide you.

Psalm 48:14 → *God is our God forever, and he will lead and* **guide us** *all the way through our lives until the very end.*

And this promise:

Psalm 73:24 → *God, you are* **guiding me** *with your wise counsel and advice, and it will lead me to a wonderful outcome.*

And this promise:

Psalm 18:36 → *God, you've cleared the path for my feet so that I won't stumble.*

Those three verses contain simple but profound declarations built on God's faithfulness. So, declare them.

1. God will guide us all the way through our lives *if* we let him. We're talking about the creator of the universe being our guide. Why would we look anywhere else for guidance?

2. His wisdom and advice and counsel will lead us to a glorious outcome. Wow! (even if it's not what we were hoping for).

3. He's cleared out *all* the obstacles – the rocks, roots, and ruts that could trip us up on the path we're traveling.

Hey, what does it feel like when God is guiding us? It should feel different in some way, right? Somehow, we know it's God and not us. Little things and big things happen that feel like God-produced serendipity. We'll feel a deep sense of peace because we know it's the right thing. That's guidance from God.

But here's the question: Will you trust what those verses say? What will make those promises real in your own life? → Will you believe that God will personally guide you? That he'll personally advise you as you go? That he'll bring you to a glorious outcome? And, that he'll clear out all those obstacles? God said he'll do it, so believe him. If you do, it will take the weight off your shoulders in terms of trying to figure out which steps to choose next on your journey.

Remember this, though: Don't ask God to guide your steps if you're not willing to move your feet. Sometimes we get so tired from trying to figure out what direction to go that we don't feel like taking the steps once God shows us what they are, especially if it involves a bit of effort or challenge on our part. Don't make that mistake. That's a *blessing-blocker*. You asked for guidance. He gave it. So, start walking.

Here's a <u>promise</u> that will help us when we're burned-out and it seems too hard to go on:

<u>Isaiah 58:11</u> → *God will <u>continually</u> lead you and guide you as you go, and he will satisfy your needs when you're in that dry parched land, giving you <u>renewed strength</u>. In fact, you'll be just like a well-watered garden, <u>like a spring that never goes dry</u>.*

What's in this promise for you? → **3 things.**
1. God promises he'll guide you and lead you <u>continually</u> as you make your way along the path you're on. **Are you going to believe it and rely on him for it?**
2. When you feel worn out, and tired, and dried up, God will refresh you and give you <u>renewed strength</u>. **Are you going to receive it from him?**
3. You'll be like a lush garden that has plenty of water, like a spring that continually produces refreshing water. Instead of parched and dry, you'll be <u>refreshed and well satisfied</u>. **Are you going to be like that?**

What's it going to take for that promise to become personally real in your own life? Don't just read this and move on.

I suggest **ABC**'ing it over and over again until it becomes real to you, and then sit back and watch with confidence, trusting God to come through. It's his desire to do so. He loves it when we unconditionally believe his promises <u>with child-like faith</u>.

<u>But just remember</u>: Don't ask God to guide your steps if you aren't willing to move your feet.

Sometimes, it seems like we just can't see the path ahead of us. There's no direction in his Word and we don't hear God speaking to us. <u>We're just stuck.</u>

It's been said: *He who does not understand God's silence will not understand his words.*
Are you taking God's *still small voice* as silence...or... guidance? Often, he speaks with a *soft whisper* (see 1 Kings 19:12), and when that happens, <u>some of us just might need some hearing aids.</u>

Here's what we need to remember, so put this in your backpack → God <u>already knows</u> what's up ahead before we do. Sometimes all we'll get from him is a soft whisper – <u>one tiny step</u> to take. That's all...just one tiny step. And since it's not the great revelation we were expecting, we can easily miss it and end up missing out. It's failing to take that one tiny step that gets us in trouble. **But there's a reason for that small single step.** God in his wisdom knows that's all we can handle at the time. So, we need to put out our foot and just take that one tiny step. Then he'll give us another and another. You get the idea.
<u>Even the smallest of steps will move you forward.</u>

Look at this <u>promise</u>. Yeah, yeah I know...we're covering it again! ☺

Proverbs 3:5,6 → *Put your trust in God with everything that's in you. Don't just rely on your own understanding or your own judgment in each situation. In all your ways* (your plans, your paths, the decisions you make), *acknowledge God* (invite him into the middle of your situation). *Do this and he will guide and direct your steps, smoothing out the way for you, and levelling out your path.*

I think many of us get stuck in relying too much on our own judgment when we make plans and decisions in our lives. We forget to invite God into the mix. So, who ends up directing our steps? We do...and that can get us into messes.

And, to make things worse, when things aren't going our way, we push harder on that door that God is maybe closing. This is where many people miss out on God's blessings – when he closes that door it's for our own good. He has other blessings in store for us. It would be foolish to manipulate the circumstances just to force that door back open. Either God's in control...or...we are.

Here's a promise that goes along with what we're talking about here:

James 1:5&6→ *If you need some guiding wisdom, then ask God and he will give it to you. He won't look down on you for asking. But just make sure you ask with faith, no wavering or doubting God's willingness to help you.*

Want some wisdom and guidance in the decisions you have to make? Then the first source to go to is God. But there's a contingency.→ Ask with no doubting, no wavering. Yet many of us are disappointed because we didn't receive the wisdom and guidance *we wanted*. But, *if* we're asking *with absolute certainty* that we will receive it, then the wisdom and guidance from God will be just what we need. It may not be what we wanted, but it will be what we needed. Can you accept that?

Here's one of my 'life- verses' on guidance.

Psalm 32:8 God speaking→ *I, God, will guide you along the paths you should choose* (meaning - I will make plain and show you the roads you should travel on, the decisions you should make, the course of life you should follow). *Along the way, I will instruct you* (meaning I will give you insight into your circumstances) *and I will teach you* (meaning -

plainly point the way out as if by aiming a finger) *and I will advise you as you go. And, my eye will be upon you, <u>to watch over you</u>* (to make sure you're safe and staying on the right path). ***<u>But, make sure you don't act like a resistant horse</u>*** *that lacks understanding, and needs a bit in its mouth to keep it under control or else it will not come with its owner.*

Yes, it's a long verse, but don't let this passage slip by.

<u>There are 5 promises God makes to us in that verse.</u>

1. God will <u>show us</u> and <u>make clear</u> to us the paths we *should* choose. (That's what we all want, right?)
2. God will <u>guide us all along the way</u> so we're not alone, nor directionless. (He won't quit on you halfway through)
3. Along the path we're on, he promises to <u>give us insight</u> and understanding into our circumstances, so we don't mess up.
4. Along the road we're traveling, he promises to <u>point out the way,</u> as if by aiming with a finger (so there's no confusion).
5. Along the entire journey, he promises to <u>watch over us,</u> to protect us, and make sure we stay on the right path (just as if we had a personal guide and bodyguard).

Think about it → What more could we ask for if we're seeking the very best therapy, guidance, or counseling that money can buy...but without the price tag? Definitely **ABC** this one.

<u>A</u>= <u>A</u>gree with what God that he's the guide, not you.
<u>B</u>= <u>B</u>elieve in your heart he will do all those things in that verse.
<u>C</u>= <u>C</u>onfess it to yourself and others (whether in your heart or out loud) to feed your faith and starve your doubt.

But why did God add that last part in that passage...about the resistant, stubborn horse that lacks understanding? I'll tell you what I think. Sometimes the path God's chosen for us is not the path we want to travel on. And because we lack the understanding that it's the *best* path for us, we resist, just like that horse.

Here's a key point, so put this in your backpack for your journey through life.→ It's the clincher to that promise we just covered:

Have you ever seen those barrel racing horses? They're turning this way and that way as if they know exactly what the rider wants. All the rider has to do is gently nudge the side of the horse with his heel and the horse will go in the direction its owner wants. **We need to be just like that** – so sensitive to God's nudges that we understand which direction he wants us to go. There are two things involved to make that happen:

1. Being able to recognize God's nudges.

2. Cooperating with God, not resisting him in the direction he's trying to get us to go. You don't want God to put a painful bit in your mouth, so to speak, just to get you to go his way, do you? Ouch!!!

Those 2 principles are a major part of what guidance from God is all about. Use them and you can't go wrong.

🌲**I like this follow-up promise that seems to go with that previous verse:**

✦ Isaiah 30:21 → *If you leave God's paths and go astray, you will hear his voice behind you saying to you, "No, don't go that way, go this way."*

Notice that it's 'God's paths' not our paths that it's referring to. When we stray away from *his* path, then it means we're walking on our *own* path. God knows that could lead to problems and that's when he steps in to protect us by speaking to us, reminding us to get back on his path.

The question is, are we listening? His path is *always* the best, leading us toward the good things he longs to give us. So, don't leave it. Put on your hearing-aids and listen for his voice.

And notice it's God's voice we should hear, not a friend's voice, or a therapist's voice, or the author of a self-help book's voice. They can all be helpful, but the voice we should be hearing most of all is God's voice. Are you doing that?

What if we miss God's voice? Well, that could lead to problems. We need to be able to hear him or we might *keep* walking down the wrong path and that could spell trouble. Obviously, we've made the choice to veer off onto a different path because we thought it was better and would make us happier. Well, it just might make us happy, but it probably won't be the happiness that comes from the blessings God intended for us, and that's what we'll miss out on. It's definitely a *blessing-blocker*. **I have done that many times. Don't you do it too.** ☺

If we're keeping God in the forefront of our day, talking with him about the little things and the big things in our lives, we'll be able to hear him better. If we don't make a place for God, he won't push his way in. If we're checking our social media or watching tv, we probably won't hear him say to us, *'Shut that thing off, I have something to say to you.'* He'll just wait until we draw near to him before he speaks. So, determine that you'll keep God before you throughout the day, listening for his voice and feeling for his nudges. And again...put on your hearing aids.

<u>You might be thinking</u> → *"I feel like I'm always in the dark; like I'm walking blind. I don't even know if I'm on God's paths."*

If you feel like that way, then read this last guarantee in this section. It's amazing!

✸ <u>Isaiah 42:16</u> → *I, God, will <u>lead</u> the blind along a path they're unfamiliar with, and I will guide them along <u>a road they haven't traveled before</u>. I will make the darkness they're in become <u>light</u>, and I will turn the <u>rough paths into smooth terrain</u>. This is what I will do for them. I will not abandon those who are mine.*

Yeah, I underlined a bunch of words again, <u>but don't miss this</u>. Are you God's child? Then, take him at his word. This verse is directed at you. He says this is what he wants to do for you:

- **If you feel like you're walking blindly with no direction**, God will walk with you, leading you. He promises to do it.
- **If you feel like you're stuck on the path you're on**, God promises to lead you down a *new* path, one you haven't travelled before. And you know if it's God leading you, it's going to be a good path, with good things along the way.

- **That darkness you feel you're in?** God will turn it into the *'brightness of day'* (that's what the Hebrew word for *'light'* means in that verse). You'll be able to see your way clearly. You'll go from confusing darkness to the bright light of day.
- **If you feel the path you're on is pretty rough and hard to travel on**, God promises to smooth it out (the Hebrew word for *'smooth'* means to straighten it out and make it flat and easy to travel on). Who doesn't want that, right?

<u>Bottom line</u> → God's paths are well lit and easy to travel on, and he'll personally be your guide. It's what he loves to do. He wouldn't have said it over and over again in his Word if he didn't mean it. So, take him up on it. Hire him to be your guide. Like I said...you can afford it...it's free!

Don't Get This Wrong:
So, what are you going to do with that verse we just covered? <u>Are you just going to read it and then move on</u>? In my opinion that would be such a waste of opportunity. Think of all of the guarantees we just covered in this section...the guidance, the counsel, the wisdom, the protection, the successful glorious outcome. Why not take God up on these things? He's the one offering them to us. What do you have to lose? It's yours for the taking. Receive what God says he'll do for you and live it out in your life. **That's what living by faith is all about.** The choice is yours to make. Whatever you decide, it will make the difference between an easier life...or...a harder one.

Again, God makes his way of living simple,
but we...we seem to make it hard.

PRAYER
What God Promises Us

"The greatest tragedy of life is not unanswered prayer, but unoffered prayer." F.B. Meyer

I'm sure it comes as no surprise that the reason we pray to God is that we want God to hear us. Many people think that God should *automatically* hear them when they pray.

I have found that when I ask people if they think God has any requirements or expectations for answered prayer, I usually get a blank face. So, I thought it would be good to go over some promises that we may need to know *if* we truly want our prayers answered.

One thing's for certain. When you read the following promises, you'll find that God is really clear that he *wants* us to ask him for things. He keeps telling us to do so over and over again. You'll see what I mean. Read on.

We have a God who wants to give us anything.

Matthew 21:22 Jesus speaking→ *You may ask for <u>anything</u> in prayer, and if you <u>believe</u> and have faith, you will receive it.*

Anything? You mean anything? Obviously, this is not a *'genie in the bottle'* promise, yet I sometimes think we treat it that way, as if God only exists to fulfill our every request. After all, he does say, *"You may ask for anything."*

The key in this verse, though, isn't the freedom to ask for *anything* we want...it's the word **'believe'**.

The other key is **'motive'**. Get those two right and God will answer your prayer. That's what he says he'll do.

And think about this, if we truly believe that the will of God would be the best outcome for our lives, then we'll ask for things in harmony with *his* will...not ours. Wasn't that what Jesus' motives were behind his prayers – God's will?

Here's an important promise relating to prayer:

Mark 11:24 Jesus speaking→ *I tell you the truth, whatever you ask for in prayer to God, believe that you have already received it, and it will be given to you.*

Don't miss this important criterion for prayer. Do you believe you've *already* received what you've asked God for? If you do, then that's sure proof of your faith, isn't it? I often find myself asking for something and then forgetting about it throughout the day. It just shows that I had little faith that God would answer me. However, if I had truly believed it was in agreement with God's will, and that I had *already* received it, I doubt I would have acted that way. I'd be *expecting* with certainty for God to come through. How about you?

The power in his name.

John 14:13 Jesus speaking→ *If you ask from God anything in my name, I will give it to you, so that it will bring honor and glory to God through me.*

Jesus keeps telling us in different ways to ask for *anything*. I think we sometimes limit God by *not* doing that. So, why not ask? Let's ask for the impossible. See what happens. After all, if we're asking for the right stuff, it gives Jesus the chance to bring glory to God and people will see that we're blessed by God.

But whatever you do, don't miss this point:

Too often people will quote that promise and leave out the last part. Yes, we should ask God for things with the authority of

Jesus' name, but then in the next sentence Jesus immediately tells us that if we truly love and care about him enough to ask for things in his name, then we should obey his instructions and commands. → *For if you truly love me, do what I tell you to do, obey my instructions and commands. (See verse15)*

Sometimes I think we don't want to hear that part. Why? Because now that promise becomes much harder to live out. But, lucky for us, God's Holy Spirit lives inside us, continually giving us the power to obey Jesus' words. (See Philipians 2:13).

Here's another thing worth mentioning. → It's interesting to hear people end their prayer with the all-familiar formulaic, **"In Jesus name, amen."** In fact, it almost feels uncomfortable if we don't hear it at the end of a prayer, right? But have you ever asked yourself why we pray in Jesus' name? I mean, if you look at all the prayers in the New Testament, not one of them ends with the words, *"In Jesus' name, Amen"*. So, why do we say it?

When Jesus says to ask in his name, he doesn't mean for us to just say those words, *"in Jesus' name"*. He means for us to approach God with his authority backing us up.

When the police on TV used to say, *"Open up in the name of the law!"*, they were claiming their demand was backed by the *authority* of the law. So, for us to ask God for something *in Jesus' name*, we're asking with the *authority* Jesus gave us to rightly come before God with our request since we're living under Christ's Lordship. But it's going to be hard for him to back up our requests if we're not living in obedience to his commands. Think about it, if we move out from under Christ's Lordship (wilfully doing our own thing instead of God's), then how can we ask God for things with Christ's authority behind it?

Wanna know something else? God's not interested in how fancy our prayers are, nor how long they are. He'll answer three-word prayers, like *"God, help me!"*, just as willingly as he does those long drawn-out prayers. Don't forget, he *already* knows what we need before we even ask him.

✦ **Matthew 6:7&8** Jesus speaking → *When you are praying, don't just babble on and on, or use meaningless repetition like some people do. They think God will hear them if they do so.*

Don't do that. After all, God your heavenly father <u>already knows</u> what you personally need even <u>before</u> you ask him.

When you think about it, it's not the words that matter so much, but rather the motives and the faith behind the words that God is looking at. Right?

Are you asking in <u>agreement</u> with his will for you?

1 John 5:14,15 → *This is the <u>confidence</u> we have when we approach God in prayer. If we ask anything that <u>pleases him</u> and is <u>in agreement with his will</u>, then <u>we can be sure</u> that he has heard us. And, if we know that he's heard us, then <u>we can be sure</u> that he will grant our requests.*

Wanna be sure God <u>*hears*</u> your prayers and <u>*answers*</u> them? Then follow that verse above (along with the others).
Here are the **3 criteria**:
1. Ask for <u>things that would bring God pleasure</u> in giving them to you.
2. Ask for <u>things that are in agreement with his will</u>, since he knows what's best for you.
3. Check to see if you have the <u>confidence and certainty that God heard you</u>.

Add these 3 things to your 'prayer criteria' and according to this promise, you can be certain to get what you ask for from God.

Abide & Remain. How about this next promise:

John 15;7 Jesus speaking→ *If you <u>abide</u> in me* (meaning, remain close to me, in a deep relationship with me) *and my words remain in you* (meaning, you remember them and do what they say), *then ask for <u>anything</u> you want, and it will be given to you.*

Here are 2 more criteria for our prayers to get answered:

1. **Abide in Him**. You might be wondering what that means. It simply means to remain close to him through good times and bad (staying within the sphere of his love, his care, his will, his blessings, and his protection etc.). Too often we seem to draw near to Christ in the good times, in moments when we feel emotionally connected to him. But when circumstances get tough, we can tend to move away from him rather than draw closer. Don't let that happen. That's a *'blessing-blocker'*. Just remain _in_ him in every situation.

2. **His Word needs to be abiding in us**. This simply means his instructions need to remain with us, not ignored or forgotten, or taken casually, but instead, they're leading us to live our daily lives in agreement with them.

Notice the word '_then_' in that verse we just covered. It's an adverb. It usually indicates what comes next. If you do this, _then_, that will happen. Example → If we're remaining close to him and his words live in us, causing us to do what he instructs us to do, **_then_** we can ask what we want from God and receive it because it will be in agreement with his will. **It's like a key that opens a door**. Having the right key matters.

Look at this promise: Don't forget to do this.

1 John 3:22 → *We will receive from God whatever we ask for in prayer because we do exactly what he tells us to do* (we obey him), *and we do what is pleasing in his sight*.

Again, if you want to receive whatever you're asking for from God, then do these 2 things:
1) Do what he tells you to do.
2) Do what's pleasing in his sight.

You might be thinking → *"Wait a second. Aren't those two things one and the same?"*
Not really. The first refers to what God expressly tells us to do. The second may not have a command behind it, but we know it's the right thing to do and that it pleases God.→ Example: Helping a little old lady cross a busy crosswalk may not be a

command, but it's the right thing to do. I know, I know...it's kind of cliché (helping a little old lady cross the street), but you get the idea, right?

 Here's a guarantee with a major <u>contingency</u>:

 1 Peter 3:12→ *God sees and notices those <u>who continually do what is right</u> before him, and because of this, <u>he pays attention to their prayers</u>.*

We can take this as a promise. Simply put, *if* **we want God to pay attention to our prayers**, then we need to make sure we're doing what's right before him. How do we do that? **Two ways:**
1) Find out what God wants us to do by reading/studying His Book of Instructions...his Word...the Bible. Then do it.
2) In those gray areas, where there's no clear instruction in his Word, do what we think would truly make God happy.

 Wanna get powerful results from your prayers?

 James 5:16→ *The prayer of a <u>righteous</u> person* (one who <u>continually does what is right in God's sight)</u> *is powerful and produces great results.*

We can be sure our prayers will produce powerful and effective results *if* we're living in a way that is *righteous*. That word '*righteous*' sounds intense, doesn't it? It simply means to do what's '*right*' before God. If we're consistently doing that, then guess what? → Our prayers will have powerful results.

 <u>Summary of all the contingencies God lays out about prayer</u>:
If you want God to <u>hear</u> your prayers and <u>answer</u> them, then do these <u>7 things</u>:
1. *<u>Believe</u>* that God will come through for you and give you what you ask for.
2. Believe that you've *<u>already</u>* received it.
3. Ask with the *<u>authority</u>* of Jesus' name to back your request.
4. Make sure what you ask for is in *<u>agreement</u>* with God's will.

5. Make sure you're *remaining* in him, and his words remain in you (that they're alive and working in you, producing fruit).

6. Make sure you *do* what he tells you to do (obedience to his Word), and in those gray areas, do what will please God.

7. Continually do what's *right* (according to God's instructions) – it's called '*righteousness*').

All we have to do is RAP it. Remember that one? → **RAP** = **R**ead it. **A**pply it. **P**ractice it (over and over again).

One last thing and it's worth adding to your backpack:
Just remember that everything is possible with God. So, be bold with your asking. Nothing is too hard for him. Remember these?
Matthew 19:26 → *With humans, things may be impossible, but with God, he can do anything. Everything is possible with him.*
Luke 1:37 → *With God, nothing is impossible.*
Genesis 18:14 → *I am the Lord, your God. Is anything too hard for me?*

And don't forget → Prayer is bringing our cares and worries to God. Faith is leaving them there.

Final Comment

Why did God even bother to make promises to us? What was his purpose in doing so? Could it be that God gave us promises so we would understand his intention to bless us and give us good things; that we would understand his love for us, demonstrated by the good things he wants to do for us? I think so. His promises help us in walking-the-walk of God.

Here's what I want you to think about.→ Without God's promises, our faith would have no value. Without our faith, God's promises would have no value. God's promises are activated by our faith, and our faith is energized by God's promises.

Just Remember → God loves us more in a moment than anyone could in a lifetime. He…wants…to…bless…us. He can handle any hurt…habit…or hang-up we may have, and he uses his promises to help us.

Thank you for joining me on this journey. I hope this book gave you more hope, more strength, and more faith than when you started reading it.

If so, then I would be privileged to receive a short review from you on Amazon or Goodreads. **Why?** Because many people will choose to read a book based on its reviews and I would for them to read GOD's GUARANTEES.

Just go to the last two pages of this book for how to do it.

**Again, as a way of saying thank-you
for taking the time to read this book,
I'd like to give you that gift I mentioned earlier.**

**I don't want you to miss out on it, so here it is again.
Go to my landing page and copy and paste**
www.walkingthewalk.us *(.us not .com)* into the **URL** section at the top of your computer screen.

Then click on **Gift To My Readers,** to receive my special gift that goes hand-in-hand with this book.

It will also put you on my update list to update you on other writing projects I'm working on. You can opt-out anytime.

Also, I would love to have the chance to hear from you.
You can message me at → *gkwalkingthewalk@gmail.com*

Please See The Epilogue On The Next Page

EPILOGUE

Who is the evil-one anyway...and what's he got against us?

I don't want to take up a lot of space on this topic, but I think it needs to be covered. It's important we understand our enemy and from my conversations with many believers, their knowledge of their spiritual enemy is often weak, allowing them to be bullied and beaten up by the evil-one and his minions. **So, don't miss this section or pass it by. It's critical.** Let's start with this:

What are angels? → The Bible says they are spirits created by God to minister to him and to us, and to carry out his orders in the administration of his creation.

The Bible calls the <u>devil</u> a fallen angel. He used to be called Lucifer, which meant *'light-bearer'*, until darkness and evil was found in him; then his name was changed to Satan which means *'adversary'*. The Bible says he was an archangel, high up in the hierarchy of God's angelic order, a leader of the millions of angels under him. Because of his magnificent appearance, wisdom, high position, and authority among the angelic beings in heaven, arrogance filled him with the desire to be like God; to have his own throne, and be worshiped by the angels who admired him and were under his authority. He led a rebellion in heaven, convincing about a third of heaven's angels to follow him. God immediately put an end to that rebellion and cast Satan and his minions (often referred to as 'demons') out of heaven.

Why would angels rebel against a good and loving God? Because God created them with a free-will. They were able to make their own choice to obey God's will or their own. Hence, they bought into Satan's deceit and were led by him into a great rebellion against God.

If you want, you can read about Satan's history in these Bible passages: Isaiah 14:12-14 and Ezekiel 28:13-19.

Some people think that Satan is God's evil equal. That's not true. 3 Reasons why:

1.) Satan is **not omnipresent**, meaning, he can't be present everywhere like God can. Nowhere in the Bible does it say he can. And, most likely when we're attacked spiritually, it's not Satan himself, but probably fallen angels that follow him and his directives.

Note: There is apparently an echelon of angels. Not all angels are the same. The Bible refers to them as spiritual <u>rulers</u>, different <u>authorities</u>, and various <u>powers</u> of darkness in the unseen realm. Some angels rule over nations. Some angels are appointed to protect us and minister to us. Some are created to minister to God alone.

2.) Satan is **not omnipotent**, meaning he's not all-powerful like God is. Yes, he's powerful, but he is not all-powerful. There are, in fact, limits to his power. We see that in the New Testament when Jesus would deal with Satan or his demons. He ordered Satan directly to leave him alone, and he ordered the demons to be silent or to flee from an afflicted person. We also see it with Christ's disciples when they were sent out to share the Good News about Christ. They were able to command Satan's demons with their words by the authority Jesus had given them.

3.) Satan is **not omniscient**, meaning that he doesn't know everything like God does. Satan is a spiritual being created *by* God. He knows nothing of God's thoughts or plans unless God reveals them. He is constantly surprised and caught off-guard by God's actions.

However, Satan knows our tendencies, our weaknesses, and the areas of temptation we may be prone to. He's had a long time to study them. The fact that he knows about us is *not* because he can read our minds, but because he's a master at studying our behavior.

So, basically, Satan is *not* like God.

He was created *by* God to serve God's purposes in heaven. But, because of Satan's rebellion, God cast him from his glorious position in heaven and pronounced a judgment of eternal doom upon him and the angels who followed him (See Revelation 20:10). Satan has been God's enemy ever since. He knows he's eternally doomed and that his time of freedom is limited, so he's on the rampage, lying, and deceiving, and hurting God's creation with as much fury as he can impute.

That's why Jesus called Satan *"the evil one"* the *"originator of lies"* and *"the thief that comes to steal from us, and destroy our lives, and if possible, kill us.*

God said in 1 John 3:8, that one big reason Christ came to earth was to destroy the devastating workings of Satan.

So here is a very important question:

* What do you think Satan wants to **steal** from you? → Your peace, your joy, your strength, your blessings, your success, your family?

* What do you think he wants to **destroy** in you? → Your faith, your trust, your hope, your joy, your happiness?

* What do you think Satan wants to **kill** in you? → Your relationships, your health, your life?

Don't miss this → What do all the promises of God give us? They give us a way to combat Satan. They are <u>our weapons</u>.

✦ Psalm 91:4 says→ *God's words of truth* (including His promises) *is our armor, our shield, and our protection.*

What did Jesus do when he was attacked by Satan and tested in the wilderness? → He used the <u>truth</u>. He came back with the statement, *"It is written...*" Then he would quote God's Word. He used the Word of God, which is "<u>truth</u>" as a weapon against Satan and his lies. In fact he used nothing else but God's truth as his weapon of choice. And what did Satan do? He fled.

Did you know that when the apostle Paul told us to put on the <u>armor of God</u> (See Ephesians 6:10-20) in order to protect ourselves against Satan's tricks, schemes, and attacks, he mentions defensive <u>armor</u> like the *'belt of truth'*, and the *'shield of faith'*, the *'breastplate of righteousness*, and the *'helmet of salvation.* But the <u>only *offensive* weapon</u> he mentioned to fight against Satan was the '<u>Sword of God's Spirit</u>', which he said is <u>the Word of God</u> (See Ephesians 6:17).

So, what are you and I going to do? → You got it. Wear God's amor and use God's sword – his Word (and his promises), as a weapon against Satan, the evil-one, our spiritual enemy, the one who wants to ruin our lives.

We're going to back it up by **ABCD&E'**ing and **MAC'**ing and **RAP'**ing all those promises until we see the enemy leave us alone, just as he did to Jesus when he was tempted and attacked in the wilderness.

<u>**Just to remind you:**</u>
ABC, D, and **E** stand for:
Agree with what God says in His Word is best for us.
Believe His promises in our heart.
Confess it to feed our faith and starve our doubt.
Do what God tells us to do in His Word.
Expect God to come through with what He says He'll do.

MAC stands for: **M**ake **A** **C**hoice

RAP stands for: **R**ead it, **A**pply it, and **P**ractice it.

So, let me ask you this → What's one of the main reasons we need to know, believe, and confess God's promises?

✦ **2 Corinthians 2:11** → ...*so that* we would <u>not</u> be outwitted, outsmarted, or exploited by Satan, our enemy. For we are quite <u>familiar</u> with his schemes.

God's 'promises' counter all the enemy's schemes. They expose all the enemy's plans to rob us of peace, to drain us of strength, to strip us of guidance, to steal our joy. Are you <u>familiar</u> with the enemy's tricks and schemes in your own life?

Wanna know how to effectively handle the attacks Satan hits us with?

Philippians 4:13 → *I can handle anything that life throws at me, by relying on Christ who gives me his supernatural strength.*

I know that seems almost cliché, but it's the truth. I don't think we can handle life on our own without exhausting ourselves. If we rely on Jesus' supernatural strength he gives us, we'll be ok.

One desire God has for us is to live a victorious life.
Some of us don't feel very victorious and we may not know what to do about it, so we kind of live in a state of limbo...not really fighting for our faith...and...not really giving in to the enemy either. **Here's the way to be victorious:**

1 Corinthians 15:57 → *Our 'victory' comes through Jesus Christ.*

Yeah, I know. You've heard that one before too. Another cliché. But that word "*victory*" in the Greek means to utterly vanquish, to have total triumph, to crush and trounce your opponent. And we know who our opponent is, don't we. It won't happen automatically. It will only happen *through* remaining in Christ.

You might be thinking → *"I'm still confused! How exactly does 'victory' come through Jesus?"*

The victory came by Christ destroying Satan's power over us.
1st John3:8 says the Son of God came to destroy the workings of the evil-one, right?. Well, how did he do that?
Through The Great Exchange:
He took our *sins* upon himself, and he gave us his *righteousness*. That's The Great Exchange. And now, the enemy can't accuse us of one single sin, because we're no longer guilty. We're made righteous and holy, and the Bible says we've become **saints**!

The victory came through Christ's horrible death on that Roman cross. It sounds like he was defeated, but the opposite is true, and here's why:
When Jesus hung on that cross, he bore the world's sins, and he took on God's judgment and punishment for our rebellion. And because he satisfied God's judgment against our rebellion *(which was eternal death and separation from God)*, he destroyed the power that sin had over us. We're free from its grip. **And here's**

the cool part → Now that the sin-problem is solved, God can now live inside us because we've been purified and made fit for his presence to dwell in us...forever.

That was Satan's ultimate weapon against us – sin and death. He wanted to take God's judgment against our sin and use it to drag us down with him into eternal doom. He figured it was the ultimate insult to God – to utterly destroy God's creation.

But here's the thing: That *guilty* verdict God declared on us was totally satisfied when Christ took the penalty for our rebellion. God was *satisfied* with his sacrifice.

And get this: No one else could have qualified. It had to be a righteous man (*Jesus*) who died for the unrighteous – *us*.

Do you see the necessity for the virgin birth? According to scripture, the Holy Spirit hovered over Mary and there was conceived in her *"a holy thing"*. The power of God came upon her, and the angel told Mary, *"the holy thing which shall be born of you shall be called the Son of God."* (See Luke 1:35). God was spiritually and literally the Father of the child Jesus, and the child, begotten (*brought forth, produced*) by the Spirit of God, was born *without* sin...all of God in all of man.

The Saviour of the world had to be human, but he could *not* be born with a sin-nature. He was still tempted to sin, but he remained by choice, faithful to God. He had to be without sin to bear the penalty of mankind's sin – the righteous for the unrighteous. A man (*Adam*) was the key figure in the Fall, so it had to be a man (*Jesus*) who was the key figure in Redemption. Redemption means to *'buy back'*. God bought us back. We've been freed from slavery to sin. Now we're free from Satan's grasp. We're free from Hell and eternal doom. So, the victory came by Christ destroying Satan's power over us. The *guilt* of sin no longer hangs over our head. **If you think about it**, the gospel is the only story where the hero (Jesus) dies for the villain (us).

"Consider how precious a soul must be, when both God and the devil are after it." Charles Spurgeon

And here's the other thing. Through his *resurrection* from death, Christ also destroyed the power that *death* had over us. How? When God raised Jesus from the dead and made him alive again, <u>death completely lost its power</u>. Yes, Jesus died physically when he took on our sins. Why? Because sin causes death and separation from God. Jesus cried out on the cross –*"Father, why have you forsaken and abandoned me!"* But God didn't leave him in the grave. He raised him from the dead through the power of the Holy Spirit. (See Romans 8:11).

It will be the same for us. Yes, we'll die physically because of sin's effect on our bodies, but God promises to raise us from the dead, just like he did with Jesus. He'll give us new glorified bodies, ones that will never die, fit to be with God for eternity, just like he did for Jesus. **So, the bottom-line is death no longer has power over us.** Jesus defeated death and so *we* are victorious over death as well...through Jesus. We win!!!

The 2 biggies that Satan used against us were completely destroyed by Christ – <u>sin</u> and <u>death</u>. And because of that, Satan is defeated. **We are victorious over him!** He has absolutely no more power over us. None...unless we let him have it.

<u>You might be thinking</u> → *"Wait a second, I still see sin, and I still see evil, and I still see death all around me."*

I agree. It's all around us. But what's been accomplished by Christ (the destruction of sin, evil and death) is **in the spiritual realm at this point in time**, *until* God brings an end to them in this earthly realm in the near future (See Revelation 20). Right now, God allows them to persist to serve his plans and purposes to draw us to himself and his goodness.

Wanna know one of the coolest things of all? Read this verse:

✥ **Colossians 1:22** → *Now God has <u>removed</u> your sins and made you <u>completely right</u> with him, and he did it through Christ's death on the cross, so now **he sees you as** clean and blameless, without anything left to make you guilty before him.*

<u>You might be asking</u> → *"How can that be? I seem to sin all the time! How can God see me as pure and clean and blameless?"*

I get it. I don't always feel so pure or blameless; not the way God says he sees me. In fact, sometimes I'm surprised at the evil that comes out of me. How about you?

We just have to remember that God accepted Christ's death on that Roman cross as the punishment <u>we deserved</u> for all the rotten stuff we've done in our lives, and he counts it as <u>payment</u> for *our* sins. So now we're free! <u>No more sin, no more guilt</u>.

The reason God sees us without any sin is that God looks at us through his <u>spiritual lens</u>. He sees us through what's *already* been accomplished by Christ's death and resurrection – the end of sin and death. We're now righteous and have eternal life.

Even though in this earthly realm, we end up sinning a lot; in the spiritual realm our sins have *already* been taken care of. They've *already* been paid for; <u>they're gone</u>, the penalty has been removed, and so God looks at you and I as clean and pure, having no sin...blameless, without a single fault...<u>through his spiritual lens</u>. We're no longer sinners...**we're saints**!

It's the <u>only reason</u> a holy God can dwell within unholy, sinful, human beings. Through God's eyes, we are purified vessels, fit for him to dwell in. It's a *spiritual reality*!

Because I talk to many believers who struggle with guilt. Let me say it again. → **Even though we often sin**, God operates in the *'spiritual reality'* that Christ took our sins and gave us *his* righteousness – The Great Exchange. And as a result, <u>God has nothing to accuse us of</u>. Nothing! He declares us clean and righteous...fit to be in his presence and fit for him to live in us.

All we have to do now is live in that <u>spiritual reality</u> that God has declared us to *already* be in.

And if we sin, we have the freedom to immediately turn from that sin and ask God to forgive us. That's what he promises to do because the price for that sin has *already* been paid.

That's something the world can never offer. Unbelievers in the world carry around their guilt, whether consciously or unconsciously. They're never really free from it like we are.

I love this bumper sticker I saw the other day → *"God, help me to be the person my dog thinks I am."*

You know what? You are that person...through the eyes of your dog (or cat☺)...and definitely through the eyes of God as well.

You might be wondering → *"There are good people. I'm a good person. I'm not evil. Isn't God being a little harsh in sentencing people to eternal banishment from him and all things that are beautiful and good?"*

I totally understand why people would think that. I felt the same way at one time. After all, the words *judgment*, *sin*, *wickedness,* and *evil* don't sit very well with our moral compass.

However, in all honesty, if we were to measure our lives against the purity and holiness of God's way of living that he originally intended for us, all of us would fall short of God's expectations of goodness. So, yeah, all of us are kinda' rotten to the core.

And besides, God's always fair in his judgments. He wouldn't be *holy* if he wasn't always fair in his decisions. But, because he hates evil and detests wrongdoing (*sin*) and the destruction it causes, he would not be fair or holy if he just let it go unjudged.

You might be thinking → *"Well, that's just unrealistic to expect anyone to live up to God's standards!"*

The good news is God already knows that. That's one reason he sent Jesus. He wanted to show us what his standards would look like if they were lived out in a human just like us. We don't have to be *'good enough'* anymore, because God gave us Christ's goodness when we became his child.

So, the best part of all is that the 'dry board' of our lives, with all the rotten stuff we've done written on it, has been wiped clean. There's nothing on it for God to accuse us of anymore. The slate is clean. We're made pure and blameless. We need to walk in that reality. **Think about it** → It's the only reason we can come into God's holy presence. And it's the only reason a holy God can come live within us by way of his Spirit. We're clean and now fit to live with God. It's a *spiritual reality*.

I've heard people say, *"There are many paths to God and heaven. Don't be so closed-minded!"*

<u>Do you know what my answer is?</u> → *"Fine...believe what you want. God gave us the freedom to do that. But he's also made it clear that he's provided only one path that leads to him."*

Listen, I didn't make the rules. I'm just going on what Jesus said. He's the one that said there's only two ways we can go when we pass from this earth, and only one of those ways leads to his home in heaven and no one can come into God's home unless they go by way of him. And once we pass from this earth, it's too late to change our minds.

In **Matthew 12:30**, Jesus said, *"Listen, either you're with me on this, or you're against me."* In other words, either you believe him, or not. He didn't leave *any* room for *'other paths'* to God, but he lovingly lets us choose what we want.

Listen, because God is love and he's so in love with humanity, he did everything he could possibly do to keep us out of the hell he created for Satan and his minions. He never intended for us to go there.

Remember, hell was *not* created for us. There is absolutely no reason we have to end up there for eternity. But unfortunately, many people don't want to accept God's conditions for making things right between us and him – receiving the forgiveness and eternal life he offers. As a result, <u>they decide their own destiny for themselves</u>. God gives them the choice to go where they want. But it's pretty clear that *if* they want to be with him in heaven forever in the afterlife, then they need to abide by the conditions he set forth to get there. His heaven...his way.

So, I guess in the end, <u>we have to decide</u>. Either Jesus was lying about the way to get to heaven, or he was telling the truth when he claimed there's <u>only one way to get to his home</u>.

I mean, think about it. If someone invited you to their mountaintop cabin and gave you directions, telling you that there's *only* one road up and it's the *only* way you can get to his home; that there is no other way. Would you say, *"I don't believe you? I'm going to go a different way to get there."* Does that make any sense? I mean, it's his home. Shouldn't he know how to get there?

The way I see it, we better get this one right. Eternity is a long time to be wrong. **And since every one of us gets to choose where we'll go**, I would rather choose God's home in heaven rather than hell (with its absence of *all the* good things that God created)...forever. Heaven sounds a lot better. It's going to be amazing exploring God's universe (which is pretty big), learning new hobbies, and enjoying fun things to do...forever!

God made heaven with us in mind. He wants it to be fun...really fun! Trust me it will not be boring. Plus, there will be no evil, no pain, no sorrow, no hurt, no death, no anger, no hatred, etc. Just think of that! Nothing but beauty and good things...for eternity.

    That's because God is *always* good to us...*all* of the time.

Hey...I would love to hear from you anytime.
Message me at → *gkwalkingthewalk@gmail.com*

NOTE TO YOU THE READER

If this book was helpful to you in any way, I would be honored to receive a *review* from you on Amazon or Goodreads. A simple sentence or two is all it takes.

Why is it important? Because many readers make their choice to read a new book based on the reviews it has.

Plus, your thoughts matter to me. I'll make sure I read every review. If you took the time to write it, I'll take the time to read it.

Either way, I am truly grateful for the time you took to read **God's Guarantees**.

How To Leave A Review Of This Book On Amazon

2 Basic Rules:

1) The book does <u>not</u> have to be purchased on Amazon to leave a review.

2) You must have an active Amazon account.

 If you purchased this book on Amazon

7 Super Easy Steps

1) Go to **your account page** and click on **Orders**.

2) **Find the book on the order page** and click the box on the right that says **Write A Product Review**.

3) Give a **star rating** (5 stars being the best)

4) (This step is *optional*) Leave a photo of the book → (any photo of the book will do)

5) In the **Add A Headline** box → Give a simple title for your review.

6) In the **Add A Review** box → **Remember** it can just be a short paragraph or as long as you want to make it.

To help you out, here are 3 questions to answer → Put them together and you've got a book review. ☺

      1) Did you like the book?

      2) Is there one particular part of the book you liked?

      3) Would you recommend it to a friend?

7) Finally....**DON'T FORGET** to click the **Submit** button

---

If you did *not* purchase the book on Amazon

7 Super Easy Steps

1) Look up the **book title** on Amazon → <u>God's Guarantees</u> by Geoffrey Kilgore

2) On the book page....**scroll all the way down** until you see (<u>on the left-hand side)</u> - **Customer Reviews** with the breakdown of the star ratings. → Just below the stars you will see **Review This Product**. Click on the box that says **Write A Customer Review**.

3) Give a **star rating** (5 stars being the best)

4) (This step is *optional*) Leave a photo of the book → (any photo of the book will do)

5) In the **Add A Headline** box → Give a simple title for you review

6) In the **Add A Review** box → **Remember** it can just be a short paragraph or as long as you want to make it.

To help you out, here are 3 questions to answer → Put them together and you've got a book review. ☺

     1) Did you like the book?

     2) Is there one particular part of the book you liked?

     3) Would you recommend it to a friend?

7) Finally....**DON'T FORGET** to click the **Submit** button

Made in the USA
Middletown, DE
20 December 2024

67833310R00109